THE SOUL OF A DOCTOR

The Soul *of a* Doctor

Harvard Medical Students
Face Life and Death

edited by SUSAN PORIES, MD,
SACHIN H. JAIN, *and* GORDON HARPER, MD

foreword by
JEROME E. GROOPMAN, MD

Algonquin Books of Chapel Hill   2006

Published by

ALGONQUIN BOOKS OF CHAPEL HILL

Post Office Box 2225

Chapel Hill, North Carolina 27515-2225

a division of

WORKMAN PUBLISHING

225 Varick Street

New York, New York 10014

Library of Congress Cataloging-in-Publication Data
  The soul of a doctor : Harvard Medical students face life and death /
edited by Susan Pories, Sachin H. Jain, and Gordon Harper.
      p. cm.
    ISBN-13: 978-1-56512-507-0
    1. Harvard Medical School.   2. Medicine—Study and teaching—
Massachusetts—Boston.   3. Medical students—Massachusetts—Boston—
Biography.   I. Pories, Susan, 1953–   II. Jain, Sachin H., 1980–   III. Harper,
Gordon, 1942—
R747.H28S68 2006
610.7'117444—dc22   2005055590

10 9 8 7 6

WHEN THEY ASK ME, AS OF LATE THEY FREQUENTLY DO, HOW
I HAVE FOR SO MANY YEARS CONTINUED AN EQUAL INTEREST
IN MEDICINE AND THE POEM, I REPLY THAT THEY AMOUNT
FOR ME TO NEARLY THE SAME THING.

William Carlos Williams

Contents

III. Easing Suffering and Loss

iv. Finding a Better Way

Foreword

PHYSICIANS OCCUPY A UNIQUE PERCH. They witness life's great mysteries: the miraculous moment of birth; the perplexing exit of death; and the struggle to find meaning in suffering. An immediate intimacy occurs between doctor and patient. There is no corner of the human character that cannot be entered and explored. A physician's experience goes far beyond the clinical, because a person is never merely a disease, a disorder of biology. Rather, each interaction between a doctor and a patient is a story.

It has been said that all of literature can be divided into two themes: the first, a person goes on a journey; the second, a stranger comes to town. This is, of course, terribly simplistic, but there is a core of truth in it. And it is also true that narratives of medicine meld both these themes. A person goes on a journey: that person is the patient, but accompanying him on the voyage is the doctor. A stranger comes to town: that stranger is illness, the uninvited guest who disrupts the equilibrium of quotidian life. Where the journey leads, how the two voyagers change, and whether the stranger is ultimately expelled or in some way subdued give each narrative its unique drama. During the course of diagnosis and treatment, we witness moments of quiet triumph and abject failure, times when love is tested and God is questioned. There is pain and there is pleasure, joy and despair, courage and cowardice.

The essays that follow touch on these aspects of the human condition. They are distinguished by the fact that their authors are in a special limbo, no longer lay men and women, but not yet certified physicians. They are in their first encounter with the sick, learning both the science and the art of medicine, and so write about the dilemmas of their patients and the conflicts within themselves with original candor. We are paradoxically reassured by their self-doubt and deep fears, because the best physicians are those who grow to be acutely self-aware. We are also heartened by their emerging ego, for all doctors must have sufficient ego to stand at the bedside in the midst of the most devastating maladies and not flinch or retreat.

I did not have the opportunity to write, or indeed to deeply reflect, during my days as a student. Thirty years ago, there was little time or attention given to exploring the experiences and emotions of trainees during their first days at a patient's bedside. The emphasis was fully on acquiring knowledge, both scientific and practical; performance was gauged on how well you could explain a patient's disease and its possible treatments. Certainly the primary imperative of a physician is to be skilled in medical science, but if he or she does not probe a patient's soul, then the doctor's care is given without caring, and part of the sacred mission of healing is missing.

Similarly, three decades ago, there was scant focus on language, the spoken and unspoken messages we gave our patients and shared among ourselves. A doctor's words have great power, received by the sick and their loved ones with a unique and often lasting resonance. Alas, we as students quickly abandoned normal speech and took on the formulaic phrases of the wards: "Your presentation is consistent with myocardial ischemia." "Excision of the adenocarcinoma is optimally done according to our protocols." "Remission rates can be as high as fifty percent with semiadjuvant chemotherapy." Adopting stylized speech was part of entering the guild of medicine and served its purpose of shorthand transmission of information among professionals. Such communication was seen as definitive and complete and was delivered with good intentions. But all too often it was obscure in meaning to a layperson and served to truncate or even end further conversation. It also worked to limit our examination of the values and beliefs of the people before us, people seeking a solution that made sense to them as individuals. We needed to explain what all this technical information meant, not only for their heart or lungs or kidneys but for their soul. The diagnosis and the treatment were just starting points to enter into a dialogue about the emotional and social impact of their condition and what we were proposing to do about it. Alas, that dialogue rarely occurred.

Writing about our experiences and the experiences of our patients forces us as doctors to return to a more natural language, one that, while still clinically accurate, is truer to feelings and perceptions. Such writing helps us step down from the pedestal of the professional and survey our inner and outer world from a more human perspective.

There has been a growing shift in the culture of medicine, and the experiment in writing is part of that change. The experiment has already proved its worth, based on what we read here. The contributions in this volume cover a wide swath of experience and emotion among a diverse group of students at a formative moment in their lives. What they learn, and what they still seek to learn, serve as lessons for us all.

JEROME E. GROOPMAN, MD

Preface

I HAVE BEEN TEACHING STUDENTS in the Harvard Medical School Patient-Doctor course for nearly a decade. It has turned out to be very different from the classes I was used to teaching and ultimately a life-changing experience. I routinely stand in front of large groups of medical students and give lectures on the diagnosis and treatment of breast cancer. But in the Patient-Doctor course, there were just ten students in each class, and the teachers sat around a table with the students, rather than standing behind a podium. There was a syllabus, of course, but many times we left the assigned readings behind to talk about students' experiences on the wards. In the beginning, I wasn't the best teacher. It was only as I talked less and listened more that I began to appreciate how much the students could teach me. As a result, I've became not just a better teacher, but a better doctor and person.

In teaching hospitals, medical students learn as much from their patients as they do from their professors. The students learn by spending time with their patients, writing down the patient history carefully, documenting all the details of a case, and performing a full physical exam. Because they are not yet doctors, they form unique relationships with their patients, helping them to understand their illnesses and treatments and bringing their concerns and issues to the attention of the residents and doctors. Being close to the patient and new to the hospital world, the medical student can serve as a valuable liaison between the two. While the doctor might be limited to a fifteen-minute visit, the student is often the only one to sit with patients, getting to know them and their families as people, which may be the most valuable tool for working through difficult decision-making scenarios. The student is also often the only one on the patient care team with the time to read every page in all the old charts and may find an important fact that has been overlooked. I've learned to listen carefully to my students for everything they see and hear.

In addition to talking about their experiences on the wards, students in the Patient-Doctor course are asked to write about those experiences as well. This selection of essays is the product of those reflections. While some of the students will undoubtedly follow in the footsteps of successful physician-authors, most are simply writing from the heart about their profound life experiences in their new world of medicine. I am very proud of and moved by our students' honest writing—all of which provides unique insight into how young men and women grow into their chosen profession as physicians.

Yet as many of these essays demonstrate, the medical students' largest challenge is not in mastering clinical or scientific principles but rather in learning how to become empathic physicians. There's an important difference between sympathy and empathy. While sympathy implies pity, empathy denotes understanding. Learning to meet patients where they are and "walk with them" requires nonjudgmental respect and appreciation for what the patient is going through. The kindness and compassion displayed by a truly empathic physician embody the bedside manner that patients value most. Maintaining empathy while upholding professional boundaries and delivering care is a delicate balance for students to learn to negotiate.

Empathy is a difficult quality to teach by any means other than example, both positive and negative. Students need to observe experienced physicians as they sit at the bedside, hold the patient's hand, explain things carefully, examine the patient gently and respectfully, answer questions thoughtfully, comfort the family, help a patient find a comfortable position in bed, ensure adequate pain medications have been ordered, and finally help with plans for going home.

But experienced physicians can also learn from students. Unfortunately, as some of the essays here demonstrate, things don't always go as planned, and medical students will undoubtedly also see what happens when providers don't pay full attention: clues are missed, patients aren't always handled sensitively, bad news is delivered inappropriately. Seeing ourselves through the students' eyes shows us how much further we need to go.

I'd learned in my training that surgeons are expected to be

the "captain of the ship" in the operating room and must be decisive and purposeful, which can make them seem brusque. The role of a surgeon is now evolving into "team leader" rather than "captain," but having a thick skin is still necessary for survival in a tough surgical residency and fellowship. These characteristics don't always endear surgeons to medical students. As a small illustration of how students view surgeons, while editing this book of essays, I suggested that one of the student authors change his description of feedback he received after a rotation from "a surgical comment" to "a brief comment." He wrote back that he really liked the word *surgical* because "this is the way surgeons really speak: terse, pointed, surgical statements." He had a good point. And as a young surgical attending, I began to realize that the sort of efficient and technically proficient surgical persona required in a chief surgical resident was not entirely healthy and could in fact interfere with my growth as a person and an effective practitioner and teacher.

As a woman and a dedicated breast surgeon, I know that empathy and compassion are as important to my daily work as technical skill, clinical knowledge, and efficiency. The students' observations have helped me see the medical world anew, keep in closer touch with our patients' points of view, and revisit the reasons I went to medical school in the first place. I am very thankful for the opportunity.

SUSAN PORIES, MD, FACS

Introduction

My most trying weeks of medical school were spent in the emergency department at the Massachusetts General Hospital. I took call with the surgical residents, which meant I worked twenty-four-hour shifts every other day. In addition to suturing minor lacerations, I participated in trauma care. When a trauma patient arrived—often a victim of a gunshot, stab wound, or motor vehicle accident—I sent blood to the appropriate laboratories. It was a minor role, but it provided a front-row seat to human tragedy that one otherwise only hears about on the evening news. It was the kind of excitement that draws some of us to medicine in the first place.

Midnight on my third night on call, I was summoned: "Trauma team to trauma." I collected all the necessary vials and hurried to the trauma bay. The patient had arrived, and there was an urgency to the situation that I had not seen before. On previous nights on call, our patients had ended up walking out of the emergency room nearly intact. The patient on the gurney was different. Seventy-three years old, she had been struck by a car traveling sixty-five miles an hour and thrown fifteen feet. Her hips were shattered. She was losing blood faster than we could replace it.

My surgical resident called out for me to obtain a medical history from her family. He was going to take her to the operating room. I ventured out to the waiting area and saw our patient's eighty-year-old husband. I asked him to join me in a private room and tried to be concise.

I said, "Sir, I'm very sorry, but your wife is going to the operating room. Her condition is unstable, and we need some information from you about her medical history. Does she have any medical problems or take any medications?"

I had never before seen an eighty-year-old man cry. He sobbed, "No, no, no, no," over and over again. "It's my birthday. We were just getting off the bus after going to the casino. She doesn't listen to me. She just runs ahead with a mind of her own, and see what happened! Tell me she's going to be OK. Tell me!" Uncomfortably I placed my hand on his shoulder and listened to him cry, reminding myself to press on with my questions. Except for hypertension, she did not have any medical problems and was not allergic to any medications. She had been in near-perfect health. They had been married for fifty-five years.

Mrs. M. made it through the early morning but died on the operating table. There was talk of salvaging some of her organs for transplant. I went home and crawled into bed. I had been awake for twenty-seven hours. I could not sleep.

When I started medical school, I did so with the unwavering belief that I could save lives, ease suffering, befriend my patients, and go home satisfied every day. That was, at least, how I justified the costs and length of training. I was maddeningly naïve about what I was about to experience.

Caring for patients has given me much of what I've wanted from a career in medicine. I followed a critically ill man with myasthenia gravis, a debilitating autoimmune disease, from death's door to the exit door of the hospital. A patient whose laceration I sutured returned to the hospital and presented me with two neckties to thank me for caring for him. Still I was not prepared for how I might react to watching a seventy-three-year-old woman die on her husband's birthday. I did not expect the angst that I would feel about the limits of medical science or the barriers erected by our mazelike system of care. I did not anticipate the fear and guilt about the harm I might inflict on patients. I did not expect, at age twenty-four, to be so consciously aware of my own mortality. Slowly the veil of ignorance is lifting.

The political scientist Michael Walzer has written extensively on the phenomenon of "social criticism." The ideal social critic, he argues, is someone who is embedded in a society but able to apply external values to critiquing it. The medical student represents the Walzerian ideal. Knowledgeable about medicine but still idealistic, the medical student has not yet been changed by the norms of practice. He may be more able than others to reflect thoughtfully on the health care system and uncover defects in care—and more sensitive to the effects that these defects have on patients.

This book, a compilation of essays by fellow students at Harvard Medical School, chronicles our transformation as we begin to confront the reality of taking responsibility for the health and lives of patients. Many of the stories here will inspire confidence in the medical profession's youngest members. Others will raise questions about how we care for our patients. Grouped under four themes—communication, empathy, easing suffering and loss, and finding a better way—the essays collectively reflect the complexity of emotions and personal challenges that we experience as we begin to care for the ill. At their core, these essays provide a glimpse into the young physician's hopes for, and misgivings about, both themselves and the profession.

SACHIN H. JAIN

THE SOUL OF A DOCTOR

I.

Communication

Speak clearly, if you speak at all;
Carve every word before you let it fall.

OLIVER WENDELL HOLMES SR.

More Like Oprah

Alaka Ray

I HAVE COME TO SEE that in the practice of medicine the goal is not necessarily to cure people. Mostly it seems to be about doing as much as a patient will let us do. Usually that means doing a lot. Some patients want the sophisticated imaging of an abdominal CT scan, all the blood tests, and a bone scan thrown in for good measure. They dutifully take their medications and succumb to dozens of probing examinations.

Recently, however, Ms. C. from Trinidad, a retired seamstress, stayed in the hospital for six days; and when she left, it wasn't because she was any better than when she came in. She had what we called "vague complaints." She was a tiny woman who had lost thirty pounds in the last year and sometimes spit up blood. She had a pain in her neck, but if asked to characterize it, locate it, or place it neatly on our handy ten-point scale, she adamantly refused, saying, "How can you know it when you don't feel it? I don't know your pain; you cannot know mine."

We all nodded.

And so the tests began. But after an abdominal CT, a lot of blood work, a test for tuberculosis, and an HIV test for AIDS, she stopped. She just wouldn't. It was impossible to ask her to drink nasty prep for a colonoscopy, and she refused IV access for other tests. The time had come for drastic measures. We actually started talking to her. The house staff began tentatively suggesting to me after rounds, "Hey, do you think you could go see if Ms. C. will agree to this?"

But talking to her didn't make anything easier. Her view of us was not flattering, and her insistence that if she had money she would have gone to Canada for treatment left us feeling a little discomfited. It seemed unfair that we had to not only come up with an exquisitely detailed plan for her every morning but also sit and convince her of its merits—only to have her turn us down.

As my talks with her became more involved, I began to worry more and more. One afternoon in particular, I discovered that she apparently knew what illness she had. It was a cancer that had been featured on *Oprah*. Ms. C. had actually written to Oprah for more information and a spot on the show.

"Of course, they already had someone with this disease on the show, so I guess that's why I can't go," she explained.

This revelation did nothing to reassure the house staff. And when we found that the hospital chaplain had written in the chart, "Patient feels that she must go to California and find Oprah," we decided to call psychiatry, although not without wondering if we should tell the patient that Oprah lives in Chicago.

Ms. C. vehemently refused to see a psychiatrist or take any antidepressant medication, although our depression screening was positive for every symptom except guilt. Her beliefs about her body were unshakable. She didn't like what antidepressants did to her, and she didn't think we had gained the trust of her body enough to unravel its secrets.

In some ways, it was refreshing—and alarming—to realize how much most of us surrender to doctors and how vague our relationship with our bodies tends to be. Ms. C.'s ownership over her body was absolute, and when she decided to use pennies taped to her belly for pain, her lack of confidence in our science was irrefutable. As her medication chart became a long row of "Patient refused," and every test we wanted was denied, we had no choice but to discharge her, pleading with her to at least eat more and consider talking to her primary care physician.

She left, declaring to me that she would never come back to a hospital.

As my intern typed out the discharge summary, he said, "So what did we actually do for her?" The list wasn't impressive, and we had prescribed no medications. It occurred to me how deeply we depend on the patient's trust and regard and how dependent we are on compliance. Unlike school truancy laws, there is no law saying that you must submit to medical treatment. Our intentions are not actions until a patient enters into a partnership with us. At the end of the day, if we don't take the time to cross cultural, religious, and psychological barriers, we will never know how many of our patients are leaving the hospital discouraged and alienated, wishing that we were a little more like Oprah.

Learning to Interview

Joe Wright

My MEDICAL SCHOOL assigns students to interview patients almost as soon as we start, well before we know the slightest thing about the diseases the patients may have. The point is not to make the diagnosis, but to learn how to get the story with an open mind, how to connect with people about things that matter, to listen to the patient.

There were a lot of things I worried about when I contemplated medical school's challenges, but interviewing patients was one thing I thought would come easily. In my work life before medical school, I'd interviewed strangers ranging from inmates of a youth prison system to emergency-room patients. I asked people about crimes they'd committed, wrongs they regretted, the diseases they feared, and the people they loved. I'd gone up to men on street corners and asked them about the details of their sex lives, and heard all about it right there on the street. Even if I couldn't keep my G protein–coupled receptors straight, I liked to believe that I was, at the very least, Mr. Empathy.

And I wasn't bad at medical interviewing, or at least not right away. I wasn't good at it either, but that was OK. I was just having a hard time making sense of my patients' stories. Medical interviewing is a kind of detective work, except that instead of investigating deaths and injuries, you're trying to prevent them. There's generally only one person who can really tell you the whole history of a medical problem, and that's the person with the problem. A doctor has to connect the story a patient tells to the science of how the story came about and make all that into a new story. To say something as simple as "This is why you've got that pain," a doctor needs to know when the pain came, how it felt, and what else was happening at the same time.

But patients told stories that rocketed back and forth in time without warning. They told me symptoms out of order. They might tell me about two things as if they were connected, and then I'd find out they weren't, or I'd think there was no connection and then there would be. Did the patient's argument with his wife precipitate the episode of dizziness, or were these just the big events of the day, with no connection to each other except for general noteworthiness? Such questions remained surprisingly difficult to sort out.

Patients would often drop hints of other vast territories of their lives —"Of course, that was back when I was in the war"—that I'd then forget to follow up because I was so busy trying to make sense of the details they'd already told me. But I wanted the whole story, so I started writing more details down. I started learning how to put together the patient's story in a logical order in my head, even as I heard it in a totally different order. And I started redirecting patients who were wandering too far afield.

"Mr. S———," I might say if a man started moving from a story of chest pain to a problem at work, "I want to make sure that I ask you a few more questions about that chest pain."

A couple of months into this training, we videotaped ourselves interviewing the patients. The man on the videotape was me, but he was not Mr. Empathy. I watched myself writing notes furiously, only rarely glancing up at the patient. I looked up to ask short, almost curt questions, then went back to the notebook as the patient answered. I was a note-taking machine.

The worst thing: I loved this patient. Even weeks later, her complicated medical history stayed with me, as did her resilience and passion for life, and the warmth with which she talked about her family and friends. But on the videotape I looked like a sloppy-haired version of the physician I hoped not to become. I exuded a brusque sort of competence, but not kindness. It seemed to me that in only a couple of months I had gone from Mr. Empathy to Dr. Jerk.

Watching myself making notes, I thought of all the private facts of my life that I would never tell a doctor like the one I saw on the screen. If I was going to get the patients' stories and help them make sense of them and try to help give the stories happy endings, I would have to start looking up from my notebook.

The Difficult Patient

Anh Bui

SHE WAS FIFTEEN, OBESE, and full of attitude. Jessica was also my very first patient on my very first rotation of my very first clinical year of medical school. In many ways, Jessica was a normal teenager: she constantly watched TV; body piercings protruded from her eyebrows and her tongue; and fried foods seemed to be the only items on the menu that attracted her attention. In other ways, she was not so typical: she not only had severe asthma that would force her to repeat the ninth grade, but was also plagued by depression and suicidal thoughts. To top it all off, she was now here in the hospital because of a deep venous thrombosis and pulmonary embolism. All at the age of fifteen.

No one on the medical team liked her. On the charts, the doctors had written, "Hard to deal with," "She'll never do what you say," and "Not an easy one." Her pulmonologist did not want to schedule her for a follow-up appointment, preferring to pass her off to a colleague. Others nodded sympathetically when you mentioned her name. I will admit she was difficult: She had a pain threshold below ground level and took every opportunity to complain. She would not make eye contact when you asked her questions. She did not follow instructions. Watching doctors and others interact with her, I had a sense that she had no respect for them; then again, they did not seem to have respect for her.

Here was a person who obviously hated the medical establishment but ironically was completely dependent on it. Not only did she have long-term asthma problems, but the most recent evaluation had revealed that she also had the factor V Leiden mutation, causing her to be hypercoagulable, or to form clots throughout the body. Jessica had clots in her leg and lungs. She would now be wedded to Coumadin, a blood-thinning agent, for the rest of her life, along with all of the checkups and maintenance that such a medication involves. And did I mention that Jessica hated needles? She needed Ativan, a tranquilizer, just to calm her down enough for an intravenous line. She would need blood draws at least weekly to properly regulate her medication.

More and more, the hospital is designed to get people out quickly. Give the patient intravenous antibiotics. Take out the appendix. Stabilize the patient and send him home. Hospitals would be ecstatic if all health problems were short-term problems, ones that could be resolved by the time the patient was discharged. What had seemed to be short-term problems—sudden-onset pain in her legs and pain when breathing—were in reality long-term problems. Jessica would need to start that long-term care immediately, and what I had to do now was administer long-term care in a short-term-care setting. Jessica had a laundry list of issues that needed to be dealt with: her illness, her medications, how to take her medications, how to monitor herself on the medications, and what symptoms to watch for if any problems should develop on the anticoagulant therapy. But that was not the end of it. Jessica still had to deal with her asthma by avoiding triggers and consistently using her medications. Her obesity was also a major medical issue for her, and weight loss would be something that she would struggle with every day—perhaps to no avail.

Did Jessica realize all of the issues surrounding her? Would she comply with medical advice, not just in the hospital, but for the rest of her life? Many of her problems came down to behavior modification, and behavior modification could not be accomplished in one week. But that would be about the most time Jessica would spend with us. To be sure, there are hospital services that address some of these issues: social work, physical therapy, and nutrition. But can a one-hour visit daily for seven days actually change behavior?

Unlikely.

Maybe therein lies the problem. My own doubts about the effectiveness of our actions in the long term made me just like everyone else who did not want to deal with Jessica. Without some hope that interventions will work, situations become, by definition, hopeless.

Still, there were definite reasons for hope in this situation.

Sure, Jessica wasn't the nicest person. She had a foul mouth and even gave her mom the finger, but still, one could argue she was being playful. And although Jessica would never admit that she cared about others, I knew she did. She would redirect her mom toward a more comfortable chair. She would scold her brother after he made a callous remark to their mom. She would be even more sullen than normal if her mother did not come to the hospital that day. Yes, she cared. And I could imagine this year not being very fun for her: She had recently been told that she would need to repeat a grade because she was sick so often. Now she was in the hospital—again—for a week. Nurses came by to wake her up every four hours to take her blood pressure. And it hurt for her to breathe.

As she did not enjoy the instructions we gave her, I tried to impress upon her their importance, one set of instructions and one day at a time. One of her most detested tasks was to keep her leg elevated. "It hurts!" she would moan, inevitably refusing to keep anything elevated. But on day four, as I paid a midnight visit (she is a night owl, like me), there she was—surfing the Internet with her leg propped up high. Of course, she made sure that I noticed. "Do you know how much it hurts to have my leg up like this? It's been up since you left me this morning, and my knee is aching!" I just had to smile. Given ten hours of elevated-leg time, I let her put it down and then sat next to her to talk, watch TV, and surf the Web.

She was just a normal teenager after all.

Jessica ended up being discharged on the orders of the attending several days sooner than any of us on the team expected her to be. I never got around to talking about many things with her, including her obesity and her depression. Although I was not able to have those conversations with her, I hope someone else does. And I hope she listens. And I hope she is well.

No Solution

Keith Walter Michael

HE HAD BEEN a rather cool and conversational patient until these last few minutes. He answered all the doctor's questions, brought up some of his own, and even made time to ask a little about the medical student. But near the end of the appointment, he grew visibly nervous.

He spoke cautiously. "You know, Doctor, this isn't my style, and I don't want to ask this, but . . . wha . . . well . . . and feel free to say no, but I told her I would ask, so I have to. See, my neighbor is an old lady, about seventy-something, and I help her do things like go to the grocery store, and I take her to Wal-Mart and help with some things around the house. Anyhow, she is really in pain and refuses to go to the doctor. I have offered to take her myself—to the doctor, to the emergency room, every-thing—but she refuses. She takes Percocet for her pain—I gave her all the ones I had left over and even had to buy her some off the street for five or ten dollars a pill. I told her today I was going to the cancer doctor, and she wanted me to ask you if you would write a prescription for Percocet. I will fill it and give it to her."

Before the patient finished asking, Dr. D. redirected the question to me. "So what would you do, Keith?"

The patient interrupted and started apologizing to me. "I didn't want to ask with you here. I was going to ask you to leave, or maybe not ask, but I just felt obligated, since I told her I would try."

"No, no, no," I responded, "I'm glad you asked. This is authentic, just how it is in real life. You're in a difficult position; it's tough." In my mind I was wishing he had waited until I was gone. The doctor was pressing for an answer, but I had no idea what to say. Regardless, I had no time to think before answering; Dr. D. wanted a response now.

I spoke slowly, trying to squeeze out more time to find the right answer. "Well," I started, "there is part of me that wants to say that if you write a prescription with his name on it, you have no control over what he does with it once it's given to him." I paused. "However, in this case we know he won't be using it, so that isn't right. Realistically the patient is not being treated with Percocet; it's only masking her pain. Ideally we need to get her to the doctor. Maybe we could go see her. How far away does she live?"

"No," Dr. D. interrupted, "we won't be going to see her. Now do I write the prescription or not?"

"Well, no," I said, "I wouldn't write the prescription. One, it's not legal, and more important, it isn't the treatment she needs. Until she's evaluated by a real doctor, she won't benefit from treating her pain with Percocet. On the other hand, clearly she must really want it if you have to buy it off the street. You're in a tough position, but still, I would have to say no."

I felt relieved, but my answer didn't help the patient at all. He was still in a predicament. Strangely enough, the patient was also relieved. He felt guilty for asking and was happy to hear he didn't have to be dishonest. Immediately Dr. D. concurred and then explained his reasoning. It was fairly consistent with mine, with one exception.

He explained, "If you had asked me for Percocet for yourself, I would have given it to you. Then you could have done what you wanted with it. But since you asked for it for her, I have to tell you no."

Later Dr. D. explained to me that you never do anything that will jeopardize your medical license. Never. While that sounded reasonable, I didn't feel satisfied. We protected the license, but the seventy-year-old lady was no better off, and the patient was probably going to have to buy the drug off the street illegally for her—or he could choose to neglect her. I felt as if we'd punished him for being honest. When I asked Dr. D., he too found it troubling. There was something disconcerting about telling the patient that if he lied about the Percocet use, we would write the prescription, so both he and the woman would benefit. Essentially we were all willing to let the other bear the burden of dishonesty, but none of us was willing to be dishonest. No one could think of an honest solution, so we decided to be content with no solution whatsoever.

Hours after the exchange, I wanted to kick myself for suggesting we "go visit" the patient someday on the way home. What a ridiculous, naïve medical student answer. Next time I would know to hold my tongue. But now I am not so sure that it was all that ridiculous. If the choices were dishonesty, no solution, or being forty-five minutes late for dinner one night, then maybe we could all benefit from a little naïveté. Being content with no solution certainly doesn't convince me I am successful in remembering what this "patient-doctoring" is all about.

An Emotional War on the Wards

David Y. Hwang

ALTHOUGH MEDICAL SCHOOL can be hard work at times, the most memorable learning experience of my first year occurred when I was a completely passive observer. Nothing that I had previously learned in my eighteen years of schooling had prepared me for it.

I had approached a medical school professor about the possibility of my shadowing doctors specializing in palliative care. At the time, I did not know much about end-of-life care, but I had an innate conviction that it was important. As a first-year student, I was both grateful and surprised that the specialist and her fellow had actually indulged my request. A few weeks later, I found myself on rounds with the fellow and an oncologist in one of the local teaching hospitals.

I followed them, both young doctors just shy of forty, into a hospital room. We greeted the female patient and her husband from the foot of her bed, and the doctors sat down next to the patient. I assumed an inconspicuous position in the corner of the room—trying to do my best fly-on-the-wall imitation—while taking a good look at the patient. Sitting up in her bed, she was completely engrossed in a coloring book, using a large set of crayons. So absorbed was she in her coloring that she barely acknowledged us. None of this behavior I would have found peculiar, if it were not for the fact that she was between thirty and forty years old. Had I not otherwise known a rough estimate of her age, I would have guessed that she was fifty, based on her haggard appearance alone.

Because the palliative care fellow had earlier given me a briefing, I was familiar with other aspects of her life. I knew that her husband was an officer with the U.S. Marines. I knew that the couple had two small children. I knew that she was suffering from cervical cancer, which had already spread to other parts of her body. And I knew that this marine and his ailing wife were possibly about to hear the worst news of their entire lives—that her kidneys were only 25 percent functional and that chemotherapy was no longer a viable treatment option.

What I did not know was how the young oncologist would break the bad news to the couple with clarity and compassion. As I watched the oncologist gather her thoughts, it occurred to me that she too was probably at a loss for the proper words. I had assumed before entering the room that as a trained medical professional, she would know exactly how to blend the hard truth of prognosis with empathy. Now, with her initial greetings aside, I could sense her uncertainty as she took a deep breath.

Contributing to the awkwardness of the situation was the fact that no one in the room was successfully making eye contact with anyone else present. The husband focused his laser-beam stare at the two doctors as the oncologist carefully began describing the extent of his wife's renal failure. The doctors were attempting to see eye-to-eye with the patient as the oncologist continued to explain why no more treatment plans were available and why the palliative care doctor was present to discuss other "options." Despite the literally life-and-death importance of the news to her, the patient herself looked neither at her angst-ridden husband nor at the uncomfortable doctors; instead she continued to focus on her coloring book, giving no sign of comprehending anything the oncologist was saying. Nothing going on in the hospital room seemed more important to the patient than making sure she did not miss any spots while coloring.

The lack of eye contact in the room abruptly ended, however, as the husband's previously silent angst materialized into vocal anger. Both doctors turned their heads and met the marine's intense gaze as he began to yell a series of questions. Why had no one in the hospital noted his wife's kidney status before it became too late? Wasn't this hospital supposedly one of the best in the nation? Had there not been a team of doctors responsible for monitoring his wife's care around the clock? How could they have let her reach this desperate state? Why could they not cure her? Even as an observer, I became a bit frightened at the sheer force of his rage. Medical school had not trained these young doctors for the boot camp of unanswerable questions they now faced.

The palliative care fellow gave the questions her best shot. Looking directly at the angry marine, she began to explain how doctors had tried their best to monitor her kidneys but that unexpected events sometimes occur in the course of cancers. The best that the doctors could offer at this point, she continued, was to lay out all the options available to his wife so that they could make the best-informed and most appropriate decision about how to spend the time she had left. Before I could see the marine's response, the patient herself interrupted and spoke for the first time since we had all greeted her. Without looking up from her coloring book, she calmly explained that her situation was a complete misunderstanding. She was not terminally ill. She could not be terminally ill, she reasoned, because her husband was scheduled to go to Afghanistan in a few weeks to fight the Taliban. Someone would need to take care of their two children at home while he was away indefinitely. Being terminally ill was therefore not an option. The only option was to get better, and as far as she was concerned, the discussion of end-of-life care plans was a waste of time.

The marine began to weep uncontrollably. Unable to contain his shock, aware of his wife's complete denial, agonizing over the care of his kids, he cried like a child. A crying marine is much scarier than a screaming one—a brave soldier, assigned the task of protecting our nation from terrorist threats, in a complete state of hopelessness and distress. The palliative care doctor scrambled to find tissues to give to the soldier. I could see in the oncologist's face that she was both concerned and frustrated with the turn of events, her delicate explanation of the prognosis not having connected with the patient at all. And then I watched as the patient calmly picked a new color of crayon out of her box. To her, there was no reason to get upset—no one in the room was really dying.

As the marine began to gather himself together once again, he fought back his tears and politely told the doctors that he needed some time to speak to his wife alone. Both doctors nodded their heads; the oncologist told the husband that she was terribly sorry about the news, and that she would be willing to discuss questions at any time. As the doctors got up to leave the room, the palliative care fellow added that she would be available whenever they felt ready to discuss their plans.

As strange as this whole experience had been, I did not know that perhaps the strangest moment of all was about to come next. This same husband, who minutes earlier had been consumed with rage and distraught with grief, thanked the doctors for doing their job well and for giving his wife's prognosis in a humane and honest way. He said that he was very sad about his wife's situation but that he appreciated the doctors' clarity and empathy; giving bad news about patients was one of the most difficult tasks he could imagine, and the doctors had done well. As I watched the doctors thank him, I thought about how profound that comment was, especially from a man assigned to fight in Afghanistan in the coming weeks.

Since then, I have been able to shadow palliative care staff a few more times, and every patient that I have met has been unique in his or her own way. However, my first encounter with the emotions surrounding the terminally ill introduced me to the tragic ironies that arise in the practice of medicine. I will never forget hearing a grown woman talk about taking care of her children while working on a coloring book. Never again will I see marines on the news and think that these tough men are incapable of crying. As I walk around the wards of the local teaching hospitals and see patients lying in their beds, I realize that patients may pay doctors for diagnoses and cures, but they know that sometimes a doctor's care and gentle words are all that are available. Although a doctor may think that the lack of a cure means personal failure, a family member of a dying patient may see a doctor's kindness and understanding as the gold standard of the profession.

The greatest irony is that, as a complete stranger, I witnessed one of the most vulnerable and personal moments for a family that I may never meet again. As I continue to "play doctor" with my classmates as a second-year student in our case-based curriculum, I can only imagine the true stories that are behind each anonymous "patient" we discuss. To be entrusted with a role in these stories, whether as an active participant or a passive observer, gives me a sense of awe and responsibility more foundational to my becoming a physician than anything I have been taught in class.

Giving Bad News

Amanda A. Muñoz

THERE WERE FIVE PATIENTS waiting for us in the emergency department. My giraffe-size resident raced through the halls at an Olympic walking pace; I tried desperately to keep up while being careful not to twist my ankle on my clogs and fall down. The woman we saw was groaning on the stretcher, her husband apprehensive in the corner. She was intensely nauseated. We interviewed her briefly and then mashed on her belly. I started to think about what would be at the top of my list of differential diagnoses. Before I got to the third item on my list, my resident dashed out of the room. I pushed the curtain aside in an attempt to follow him, only to have him race by me in the other direction, holding a nasogastric tube.

"We're going to put this down into your stomach so that you feel better while we're waiting for that CT scan," he said. "Does that sound OK?" He was already dipping the tube in lubricant.

The woman had trouble sitting up because she was so nauseated. "I'm going to pass out. I'm going to pass out," she chanted. "I'm going to lose my water. I'm going to lose my water." She lost control of her urine all over the gurney. "I can't sit up, I can't sit up."

We yanked her up by her elbows and forced her chin to her chest, and I put the tube in her nose and asked her to swallow. She groaned, but we got it down. We jammed it into the wall suction and ran out of the room. Her husband stroked her foot as she lay silent, her eyes closed.

"Lena, sit up," he said, his voice pleading. "It's OK."

We ran to the ICU to check on our other patients. We hustled back to the ED, trying to make stealth consult visits so as to avoid the questions from the ED docs that would inevitably develop into more consults. We sprinted to radiology. Her scan showed a small bowel obstruction but also found a large mass on her right kidney, which the radiologist deemed "almost surely a renal-cell cancer." We trucked back into the room.

"You're going to have to stay with us tonight," my resident said abruptly. "There's something blocking up your intestines and you have a big old tumor on your kidney, and we have to figure it all out."

"I have a tumor? Is it cancer, Doctor?"

"We don't know yet. We'll have to talk about it later, OK?"

"Oh, OK." She closed her eyes again.

Again we ran out of the room, flipping the curtain closed behind us. I turned my head to make sure it was closed while trying not to lose too much ground behind my resident. Lena's husband stood at the foot of the stretcher, gently stroking his wife's foot while she rocked back and forth, eyes closed, groaning, with our tube in place and her new diagnosis.

As we ran down the hall toward the OR, I felt terrible. There was so much that had gone wrong about the situation. Five months of clerkships had shown me that the ideal patient-doctor relationship, taught in classrooms and acted out on videotapes, crumbles under the demands of ward work. I had already begun to place my efficiency, interests, and performance ahead of the patient's feelings and questions. Even so, I felt ashamed that we had neither listened, nor made her feel comfortable, nor prepared her in the slightest for a diagnosis that we knew she wouldn't understand.

And yet I felt hesitant to blame my resident. He was in an impossible situation; every call night, I trailed him and witnessed the volumes of patients and problems about which he would be required to speak confidently the next morning. Additionally, I saw what was said to him when he wasn't able to cover all his bases. Who could blame him for not being compassionate when he had too much work and too little time?

Neither I nor anyone on my team ever saw Lena and her husband again. A couple of days later, I wondered what had happened to her. I thought about looking up her results on the computer, or walking by her room after checking to see if she was still in house. I decided that I was too busy; there were too many other things to get done before rounds started again. I too had put efficiency before interest and was already following in my resident's footsteps.

Straight Answers

Ari Wassner

JM WAS AN OLDER MAN admitted to the inpatient neurology service around the middle of my rotation. For the past year, he had been experiencing progressive leg weakness and difficulty talking and swallowing, which his neurologist believed was due to amyotrophic lateral sclerosis (ALS, sometimes referred to as Lou Gehrig's disease). Earlier in the week, he had shown up for an outpatient neurology appointment complaining of an awful taste in his mouth. For the past two weeks, all of his food and drink had tasted terrible, to the point that he had eaten and drunk almost nothing for several days. He had become more and more depressed in the past month as the motor symptoms progressed and activity became more difficult for him. "I wish I was dead," he said. Concerned by his deep depression, suicidal thoughts, and especially his inability to take in any kind of nourishment, the neurologist had him admitted to the hospital.

I was the first person assigned to see him when he arrived on the unit. Going into the interview, I knew pretty much only what was written in the referral note, namely that the patient was a sixty-seven-year-old man with ALS, presenting with depression and an altered sense of taste. JM turned out to be a very engaging, very nice gentleman, and he tearfully described his distress over the awful taste in his mouth, which made all his food and drink taste like wet, mushy cardboard. We talked about his weakness and trouble swallowing, and he then admitted that in general, he had felt very depressed recently. When I asked him why, he said, "I'm afraid I might have ALS."

What was strange about this statement was not the reference to ALS, of course, but the word "might": as far as I knew, this man had already been diagnosed with ALS, presumably some time ago. It quickly became clear that JM had never been told of his diagnosis. As far as he was concerned, his diagnosis was still being investigated, but the specter of ALS still hung menacingly in the front of his mind. Suddenly uncomfortable with this change in the parameters of our discussion, I beat a hasty retreat and scuttled back to the office.

I looked back through the records of his recent neurology visits to see what his doctors had of late been thinking. It turned out that only a month before, JM had been described in his physicians' notes as a patient with "progressive motor symptoms." In subsequent notes, the mention of ALS became more and more frequent, culminating in a two-week-old report from an electromyogram (a test of nerve and muscle function) that declared his findings to be compatible only with ALS. Finally, the referral note for his current admission described him as a "67-year-old man *with ALS* presenting with . . ." Throughout this process, nowhere was there any record that the possibility, then probability, then near certainty, of the diagnosis had been discussed with the patient. He had effectively been diagnosed with a terminal disease more than a week earlier, and no one had told him. Not only that, but from my discussion with him, it was clear that much of his fear and depression stemmed from uncertainty about this looming possibility.

I struggled to understand why it was that of the four of more physicians he had been seeing, all of whom had apparently concluded that JM had ALS, none had actually discussed those conclusions with him. If they were convinced enough to write the unqualified diagnosis in his medical record, why did they not say as much to his face? When, or how, were they expecting him to find out this information? It seemed odd to think that the physicians were protecting JM from the diagnosis; given the distress that grew out of his uncertainty, it seemed that giving him some answers would have alleviated some of his difficulties rather than exacerbated them. Who were the physicians protecting, the patient or themselves? Whether it was the emotions involved, or the complexity and time demands of the conversation, JM's doctors had avoided telling him what was going on, perhaps in the hopes that someone else would eventually address it.

The irony was that JM was not fooled. On some level, he knew what was happening, what it meant that no one would give him a straight answer about what was wrong with him. When I checked in on him on his second day in the hospital, his first question for me was, "What is ALS?" No one had told him what he had, but he knew it was something bad—something so bad, in fact, that the doctors themselves couldn't manage to talk about it. I explained ALS to him a bit, but I still didn't tell him that was his diagnosis; it didn't seem like my place to give the final pronouncement. Or perhaps, as I later thought, I had fallen victim to the same kind of rationalization as his physicians.

As it turned out, JM was told his diagnosis during that admission. I was not present for the actual discussion, but when I visited him afterward, he was calmer than I had seen him since he arrived. He was relieved, he said, to finally know for sure what he had long suspected, and as backward as it might seem, the certainty of his terminal illness had dispelled a great deal of his anxiety and depression.

We as physicians need to be honest with ourselves, as well as with our patients, about what we are thinking. If it is certain enough to write in the chart, it is certain enough to tell the patient about, unless there are serious mitigating circumstances. Imagine if I had, after reading his chart, asked him about his ALS—imagine if that discussion had been forced upon us right then, with neither of us prepared for it. Disastrous! Patients not only can handle the truth but expect and deserve it from us: as physicians, our charge is not to protect people from the realities of their lives, but to help them understand and work within those realities to improve their lives as much as possible. As physicians we have to come to terms with our own discomfiture and make ourselves responsible for treating our patients with honesty and respect.

Of Doors and Locks

Matt Lewis

MY HOUSE KEY, a car key, keys to various buildings and rooms whose purpose and origin I had long since forgotten, all confused the key chain and made the hospital key hard to find. I struggled to locate it, and after two unsuccessful attempts (it is amazing how similar some keys look), I found the right one. With a twist of the wrist, I opened the door and entered the Faulkner inpatient psychiatric floor. It was only my second day, and I was far from accustomed to feeling trapped behind a steel wall. I could only imagine how the patients felt, stuck inside a wing of a building until a team of people they had never met decided it was OK for them to go. Freedom, it seemed to me, was far too valuable to leave in the hands of another person— regardless of the degrees on the wall.

As I stepped inside, movement seemed to define who was a care provider and who was a recipient. The caregivers moved like busy ants. With a speed born of dwindling time and countless demands, they dodged patients and colleagues, swiftly locking and unlocking doors, scrawling on dry-erase boards, dragging their patients, who moved with the ease of broken wheelbarrows, behind them. The patients meandered like impossibly huge cargo, intent only on their immediate destination, or lost inside an internal world distant from any external reality. Some would watch with suspicious eyes or slowly follow a care provider into a previously locked room, their intention driven by the individuals possessing keys. I stood like an auspicious but unimportant bit player among this complex ballet. Thumbing my keys, I picked up the pace and walked in the direction of the patient that I was supposed to see.

The door to his room was open enough for me to see in. Clothes and food were strewn across his floor. There was nothing to indicate that he possessed any means of trash disposal.

"Hello," I said.

"HELLO," he responded in a tone I had never heard used before. It was like a flat roar.

Shocked, I looked to the two nurses sitting outside his room with a plea in my eyes. They just smiled and continued about their business. Couldn't they see that I was new, that I had never encountered a soul like this? Couldn't they see that I had no clue what the hell I was doing? In my mind, they were fully aware of this fact, and the notion that they possessed some key to correcting my situation would not leave my conscious mind.

"Do you mind if I come in?" I asked, slightly unsure.

Silence.

"Can I ask you a couple of questions?"

"I DON'T FEEL LIKE TALKING RIGHT NOW."

Still, I was not to be deterred. This was my first interaction of my first clerkship.

"Can I ask you five questions?"

"NO. YOU CAN ASK ME THREE."

Success. "OK, great," I said, smiling like a fool. I pushed open the door and sat down. He was staring at me. His gaze would not be diverted, and it was immediately obvious that he was hoping I would leave as soon as possible.

"Can you tell me why you are here?"

"I WAS LOST."

"Can you tell me more?"

"I DIDN'T KNOW WHERE I WAS GOING. YOU ONLY HAVE ONE QUESTION LEFT," he boomed at me.

Right. Sure. I know, I know, I thought. This was not going as I had planned. Gathering my remaining faculties—not that many remained at this point—I came up with my final question.

"Why can't you go home?"

"I AM LOCKED UP HERE. THAT WAS THREE."

Confused and frustrated, I left to find my resident. I walked past the nurses, who grinned at me, then returned to their duties. I grabbed my keys from my pocket and opened the door into the chart room. It was small and cluttered. I went to a table and sat down in a huff. My resident walked up behind me.

"How was it?"

"I couldn't get a thing out of him."

"Paranoid schizos are hard to get talking. After some time, he may begin to trust you and open up a bit. What did he say?"

"He told me he came here because he got lost, and he couldn't leave because the door was locked."

"Yeah. He was wandering in traffic for a couple of hours before the cops picked him up. For the longest time, he wasn't sure where he was or what to make of us. Hopefully we can get him back up to baseline soon. He is pretty bad off. Such obvious negative symptoms at a young age are never a good sign. The best we can hope for is that he is able to take care of himself for a little while." She nodded, grabbed her keys, and left to speak with the attending.

I nodded my head and watched as she walked off. I was left sitting and wondering at the myriad of doors that lock behind us when we are lost. Glancing out at the patients sitting around the unit, I said a silent prayer that the people who possess the keys would always be able to find the right one to let us out again.

Reclaiming the Lost Art of Listening

Mike Westerhaus

Sitting before me was a sixty-eight-year-old man. He rested comfortably, demonstrating an unexpected ease with the environment, for a guy known to regularly skip his clinic appointments. He wore an old, felty green baseball cap to cover the few wisps of hair left on his head. A T-shirt and jeans rounded out his informal yet well-kept appearance. My preceptor had warned me that "this guy skips office visits quite often and only comes in when he's really got something on his mind."

I started my interview with him like any other. I asked about his former work, how he occupied himself during the day, and where he lived. A hint of strain in his breathing, he replied with intention, carefully choosing words to make sure that he communicated his message clearly. As he articulated answers to my relatively superficial questions, he wove in his story of illness. He confessed that in the last couple of months his appetite had gotten out of control. "I find comfort in food," he remarked, trying to make sense of his voracious eating habits.

Comfort was something he hadn't experienced a whole lot of recently. Loss had consumed much of him over the past half decade. Five years ago he'd lost his daughter to cancer. Only one and a half years ago, his wife had passed away. During her final two months of life, he had worked feverishly at his wife's bedside in their home, scrupulously monitoring her medications, changing her sheets daily, and holding her hand for hours on end. And one day she was gone. Now his sister lay comatose in a hospital after an exhausting nine-month battle against cancer.

He went on to describe how for months after his wife's death, he ate nearly nothing and lost forty pounds. Then, three months ago, he resumed eating, more than ever before. In the past two weeks, he had started urinating frequently. Could it be, he wondered, the return of his diabetes, a disease that he had reined in years ago? He felt guilty, helpless, and broken. He expressed a laundry list of other hopes for the office visit: a referral to an eye doctor, a refill of his blood pressure medication, treatment of his receding gums, and a prescription for a navel truss to reverse his "navel rupture." He spoke, uninterrupted, for nearly forty minutes after my initial trio of questions. He had arrived today as much for a chance to share his story as for a checkup.

As he unfurled his world of sadness, I found myself thinking about the art of listening. Hearing this patient communicate intimate emotions and concerns was a privilege surpassed by little else. In plain words, this man constructed an eloquent soliloquy of loss and its toll on health. And I was fortunate enough to sit as his private audience. Yet listening did not come easily. The fact that I was thinking about the art of listening while he told his story was enough to indict me for poor listening. In addition, my mind intermittently wandered from speculating about which medical issues my preceptor would quiz me on to what time I could catch the shuttle back into Boston. I offered a periodic "Uh-huh" to conceal my waxing and waning attentiveness. And even as he detailed the final weeks of his wife's life, I remember feeling anxious about how long our interview had taken.

Some might identify this patient as "one of those types who rambles on." And I might be criticized for not gently interrupting the patient and guiding the interview. And some might charge that I compromised the care of other patients by listening to one patient and leaving other patients waiting.

Yet it seems that physicians are trained to be far too "good" at interrupting patients. Research shows that on average, physicians interrupt patients eighteen seconds after starting the medical interview. I can't imagine that much careful listening occurs during such a brief episode. Nor can I imagine that patients feel appropriately listened to in such circumstances. In the case of this patient, listening needed to be the crux of the encounter. To deny him the opportunity to share his grief would have been inhumane and irreverent toward his experience of suffering. Not to mention that a failure to listen increases the likelihood that a patient won't return to the doctor.

In my third year of medical school, faculty members started

emphasizing the necessity of efficiency and rapid patient visits. We were told that we needed to become masters of showing compassion in fifteen-minute spurts. We were taught a script, complete with lines to use, important nonverbal gestures, and the appropriate boundaries for a patient-doctor relationship. On the wards, I was even advised, "The patient's history is totally worthless." I feel skeptical of this model of patient care. Will incorporation of this hurried mentality into the way I practice medicine threaten the sacredness of my future patient encounters? Or are we being taught valuable skills that will truly serve as the gateway to empathy and healing?

Later, as I directed a penlight into this patient's pupils, he suddenly burst out, "Thank you so much for listening. I haven't ever had a doctor who has listened so carefully to what I had to say." Clearly something had been missing in his previous clinical visits. Does this mean that forty minutes are needed for the patient to feel that the doctor listened? And what really does it mean to listen to the patient? I sense that to listen means not only to hear for the sake of scribbling it in a medical record but also to give the patient an opportunity to explain themselves and their illness. Listening asks something far greater of the physician than the ability to rattle off medical facts or rumble through record numbers of clinic patients. Listening demands patience and the willingness to humble oneself before the concerns and complaints of the patient. Can this genuinely happen within the pressured patient-doctor encounters dominating the health care system today? I suspect that the answer is no.

Physicians are taught to be doers. Directing patient interviews, examining the body, performing procedures, and prescribing medications constitute the bulk of the job description in today's world of medicine. Listening, perhaps seen as a more passive activity, seems undervalued and tends to get lost in the shuffle. No box exists to check "Listened" on the reimbursement form (not that I would advocate financial valuation of listening). Undoubtedly the "doer" elements form a vital part of both healing and meeting the expectations of patients. But I sense that medicine could mean and be much more for patients if time spent listening to the patient tell his or her story were prized. Might that mean longer patient visits? Possibly.

Others will write this off as the ravings of a naïve, optimistic medical student; the advocates of efficient health care will be quick to argue that longer patient visits are not "cost effective." While that may be, we cannot forget medicine's fundamental premise that patients matter most. Complaints about the frantic pace and lack of human compassion in medicine commonly fill the general public's conversation about health care. The patients who sue their doctors for medical mistakes are the same ones who feel ignored and disregarded by their physicians.

In fact I would argue that in the long run, a reinvigorated emphasis on listening to the patient would be cost effective. I suspect that greater emphasis on hearing the patient's perspective could lead to improved diagnosis, patient understanding of their illness, and patient compliance with medications and preventive practices. All of which would likely lead to a patient population with improved health and fewer patient visits, thus alleviating overcrowded clinics and reducing health care costs.

I fear medicine is moving in the wrong direction. Excuses of pressure from insurance companies and overwhelming patient loads can't make up for the lost stories and health of patients who feel they have not been heard. Thinking back to my patient in the clinic, I still wonder whether I did the right thing. Was listening to his grief therapeutic? Did I compromise the care of other patients because of the time I spent with this individual? These are questions with which I will continue to wrestle, but in the end, I sense that I did something right.

II.

Empathy

A doctor's first duty is to ask for forgiveness.

Ingmar Bergman

Inshallah

Yetsa Kehinde Tuakli-Wosornu

Women of the African ark are distinct. There is something enchanting in the way they walk, talk, sit, stand. A quiet regality to their movements, a twinkling depth to their eyes—it is in my Nigerian mother, Ghanaian tailor, Ethiopian "aunt," and Guinean braider, a thread that weaves throughout Africa, traversing country borders to enclose, like a purse string, the entirety of the continent. It is unmistakable—indeed, unforgettable.

At times, it can even be unexpected.

On the second day my of obstetrics and gynecology clerkship, I saw it. Having finished my morning operating-room duties late, I hurriedly made my way from the depths of the hospital basement (day surgery) to the ground floor (lobby) and followed the directions given me: elevator to first floor, left to Center for Women, elevator to fourth floor, left to ob clinic, second door on right. I entered, made a breathless introduction to the attendant secretary, and was suddenly, almost violently, brought to pause as I noticed the waiting room. Before me sat ten women of the diverse African ark—some cloaked in the ebony *abayas* of Islam, charcoal-lined eyes glowing against the backdrop of silken darkness; others adorned with the vibrant head ties of West Africa, swirling patterns of peaches, reds, golds, and greens sitting atop heads like crowns; some with pale complexions, others with deep complexions; some with husbands, all with child. Beholding this collage of culture and color, my heart grew quiet. I stood up straight, relaxed my shoulders, exhaled. A sweet calm settled upon me, recalling the sights and sounds, smells and tastes, of time spent with Father in Saudi Arabia, Mother in Nigeria. Looking around the waiting room, I saw Africa—my Africa—and in the middle of a Boston hospital, at a clinic for refugee women, I was at home.

My first patient was a twenty-seven-year-old woman from Saudi Arabia who came in for a routine prenatal visit. From her chart, I saw that she had lived in Angola and was currently a doctoral student at Harvard. In the usual medical-student-as-first-line offense, I entered the exam room first to conduct the history and physical. I found a quiet, *abaya*-clad woman, who on my approach smiled warmly and asked immediately, "Where are you from?" I said Nigeria, and she nodded. "My father lives in Saudi Arabia," I added, and we were off.

Our conversation wandered from Saudi Arabian shopping malls to African cuisine to the strength of the Harvard name in Africa. We talked and laughed about immigration and its difficulties, about African presidents and African roads. As we talked, I examined. Quite seamlessly, standard questions of the obstetric clinic wove their way through our conversation: Any complaints? Bleeding? Leakage of fluid? They were standard questions, but this interaction felt different: somehow, the surrounding sterility of the hospital and the typical barrier between patient and doctor had silently fallen away.

As I turned to exit the room, my patient stopped me.

"So your father is a Muslim, right?" she asked.

"No." I shrugged. "He just lives and works in Saudi."

She frowned. "So you are not Muslim . . ." She trailed off.

"No," I said, "I'm Christian." A silence descended on the room.

My patient explained that in Saudi Arabia, unfortunately, she might not be as quick to accept my services, that her family would disapprove of her interacting with a non-Muslim physician. How odd to realize that were the context different, were we in Africa—a land that both she and I hold dear to our hearts—our connection might be threatened. In Africa, where everyone is African, lines of division are often dictated by religion—the socially constructed line that a declaration of faith draws around its declarer. In America, religious distinctions are overridden by ethnic divisions—the artificial and socially constructed noose that ethnoracial identity ties around its bearer. In either context, that division can be felt both in society and (sadly) in the exam room.

It couldn't have been more than twenty seconds before the

warmth of our initial interaction returned: "Here in America, it doesn't matter that you're not a Muslim. Africans in America are one." She asked, "Are you married?" A ten-minute explanation of the importance of marriage for me, a young, bright African woman with a promising career ahead of me, followed. She talked like my mother, or aunt, or grandmother would: "Look for someone as smart as you . . . Go to every African wedding . . . Join the African cultural group at school . . . Attend get-togethers at the business school and law school, too . . . Don't forget your life and family just because you're in school." I smiled as she spoke—all of it was familiar advice.

I left the exam room smiling—and thinking. As one interested in practicing medicine internationally, particularly throughout the greater African ark, I wonder whether religious differences will affect my ability to earn the trust of, and subsequently deliver quality care to, my patients. I wonder whether there is a place for religious belief in medicine. When is it necessary to be cognizant of religious persuasion in interacting with patients, and when is it harmful? Religion, like ethnicity, is such a salient part of all of us that it should have—must have—a place in the world of medicine. How I will incorporate my religious beliefs into my career as an African—and American—woman remains to be determined. I am sure that society incorporates both religion and division into its fabric. I am equally sure that division and medicine are utterly incompatible. *Inshallah,* the reconciliation of these two truths will one day become clear to me.

Inshallah is an Arabic word meaning "God willing."

The Twelve-Hour Child

Wai-Kit Lo

SHE WAS LYING on the hospital bed in a small, curtained room in the pre-op area of the OR; she looked tired and wan. It was seven o'clock at night, and she had been at the hospital all day. Her eyes were wet; she was quiet. Her two hands rested on the curve of her lower abdomen, as if to shield it from the outside world.

Karen had come in to the hospital that morning. She had already tried for many years to get pregnant, and now, at the age of thirty-eight, after one miscarriage and three cycles of hormone therapy and intrauterine insemination, she was fifteen weeks pregnant with her first child. So when she noticed some bleeding from below, she took it upon herself to go to the hospital, to make sure everything was still OK.

That morning, her physical exam was, for the most part, normal. Perhaps her abdomen was ever so slightly larger than would be expected in a fifteen-week pregnancy, but not alarmingly so.

She had no pain, the bleeding had stopped, and she felt fine, if a bit nervous. The ultrasound revealed a healthy fetus in her uterus—the right size, the right shape, the right position.

However, there was something else that the ultrasound showed. On the left side of her abdomen, somewhere outside the uterus but very close to it, the imaging revealed a round shape with a different echoic pattern than the surrounding area. It was fixed and painless. Given the patient's pregnancy status, we ordered an MRI.

There was the pregnant uterus, with the fetal soft-tissue structures inside, curled up in a tight little ball. There was also a large mass in the patient's left lower quadrant, definitely outside the uterus and not really part of the bowels either. Funny, it looked just like the mass inside the uterus.

Then it dawned on me: I wasn't looking at a peritoneal or adnexal tumor, but at another fetus that was growing in the woman's abdomen. A follow-up ultrasound confirmed it. Karen had a viable heterotopic pregnancy: she had twins, one growing in her uterus, the other in her abdomen, both alive and well at fifteen weeks' gestation.

Heterotopic pregnancies are rare, but intra-abdominal ones are one of the rarer subtypes. And with the pregnancy at fifteen weeks, and viable, there wasn't much literature that could help us decide what to do next. I found isolated case reports from Africa and Asia, featuring termination before week eleven and healthy delivery after week thirty-four, but there was nothing comparable to our situation. Nevertheless the ob-gyn team knew that the abdominal pregnancy could proceed only at great risk to the mother and the intrauterine fetus, primarily because of the increased risk of internal bleeding.

I wasn't there when the senior resident went to tell Karen the news. But I imagine it must have been difficult for her, finding out that she had not one but two babies, and then realizing that she had little choice but to terminate one of them. How does a mother come to terms with that? I could only hope that she took some solace in knowing that the intra-abdominal fetus was a real threat to her health and that if she were to continue to carry it, she risked losing not only both babies but her own life. Still, the decision was up to her, and thankfully, she chose surgery.

The surgery went smoothly. The intra-abdominal fetus, so fragile in its little sac at fifteen weeks' gestation, was removed along with the attached placenta, with moderate but controlled blood loss. You could see all the little features—the hands and fingers, the arms and legs, and the big head—the way that you could only if you looked inside a uterus during a pregnancy. I kept glancing over at the specimen tray at the end of the procedure, half expecting the sac to move, ever aware of the weight of our actions.

After the procedure, I waited for the effects of the anesthesia to wear off a bit, then went to see Karen in the recovery unit. I wanted to ask her how she felt, what she was thinking, whether she wanted some company. In the end, I didn't have to say anything.

"It's just a miscarriage," she said. "I'll be fine." As she smiled, her hands drifted to her abdomen, right hand cradling the healthy child still growing in her uterus, left hand resting on the spot where a child had been, a child that for her had existed for only twelve hours.

On Saying Sorry

Alejandra Casillas

Ⅰт just felt really wrong.

That is really the only way I can describe how I felt after we had taken care of Ms. D. one call night during my inpatient rotation in internal medicine.

Ms. D. arrived on Friday night from her nursing home. The ninety-something-year-old black woman appeared delirious and confused. Her thin, frail body lay on an emergency-room stretcher in the hallway as we arrived. She moaned and wailed unknowingly. Thick sputum crusted at her mouth. Her eyes were closed. She could not understand what we tried to tell her. She reached for any hand nearest to her and squeezed tightly, despite her apparent weakness. Her daughter stood by the paramedics, perplexed and shocked. Ms. D.'s mental status had been perfectly fine two days ago. She had been, until now, a completely articulate and spunky old woman, known for her sparkling southern charm.

Finally, after an hour, we were able to admit Ms. D. to our service, and it became clear to me why we had not acted more aggressively when she first arrived. The intern I was working with, Dave, leaned over and explained that Ms. D. had specific wishes outlined. She would be in for treatment, but without invasive measures. No central lines, no need for an emergency ABG (arterial blood gas). We would try to make her better, try to treat her apparent infection (most probably an aspiration pneumonia), but comfort came first. Comfort *first*.

Ms. D.'s daughter made that increasingly clear to us before she left. She half-joked that her mother would run the other way if we were to chase her with a central-line needle. She knew all too well that her mother's time would come soon. After talking with us for a while, she moved over to her delirious and semiconscious mother and said loudly, "I love you, Mom. I'll see you soon. Have a good night."

What? At this point in the evening, I started feeling a weird knot at the bottom of my stomach. You know that your mom might pass away sometime soon, and you are not going to spend the night with her? If it were my mom, I would have been at her bed every single minute, not letting a moment go. I tried to check myself; I did not know this daughter's story. She probably had good reasons for leaving, had been through this before.

The daughter left, and Dave and I started to go over the plan. The associate nurse came over. Ms. D. was an intravenous nurse's nightmare—weak pulses and an impossible arm venous stick.

And no central-line option. How would we get blood cultures? How would we know how to treat this infection?

Dave proposed a third option: a femoral stick. The pulse would be better, and getting the blood would be quick. "Alej, you'll help me do it," Dave said. "OK," I replied.

"How many femoral sticks have you done?" the nurse asked.

"One," he said.

The nurse raised an eyebrow that only I caught. And afterward I knew why.

A femoral stick is not easy. And it is very painful. Dave and I proceeded into Ms. D.'s room. My job would be to hold her legs down and grab her hand as Dave stuck the inside of Ms. D.'s thigh with a thick needle. I will never forget the first stick.

"Please, no, no, please," Ms. D. wailed, wakening from her septic, sleepy coma as the first piercing went through. I bore down stronger on her skinny legs and arms as she flailed around. No blood. He moved the stick around. More screams. No blood. Needle out.

Another needle, another stick. He moved this needle around for another fifteen minutes.

Second needle out. At this point, I was almost on top of Ms. D., restraining her as if she were a madwoman, knowing she was anything but that. She looked like a meek, blind, ninety-year-old angel.

We were sweating like crazy. Dave looked disconcerted, frustrated, and angry with himself. He took the second needle out. OK, we were giving up, thank God. I could not do this anymore.

"Just one more, Alej. And if it doesn't go through, then we'll just give up and figure out something else."

What? I thought. We were torturing her, and to what purpose? We would have to start treating her with antibiotics anyway, and she would most certainly die soon! Another stick—I could not believe it.

Another needle went in. "You're almost done, Ms. D.," I choked back tears as she yelped again. She squeezed my hand. I felt like such a liar. I had been saying this throughout the last two sticks. Dave continued to fiddle with the needle. Another ten minutes passed, and finally he gave up. Three sticks later. Bloodless. An elapsed forty-five minutes of pain.

Later, Dave thought that it would be a good idea if I placed my first Foley urinary catheter into Ms. D. Oh, boy, I thought once more. Again, Ms. D. endured a second set of clumsy hands as they attempted to pull on her rigid legs, inserting that tube into her small-framed pelvis. Although the nurse could have done it in two seconds, here I was, practicing on Ms. D.

On my second attempt at the Foley, her pain finally ended for the night. That night, I did not admit a patient. I spent most of my time with Ms. D., holding her hand. She would squeeze once in a while. She kept saying she was cold. She felt like ice. She would moan, "I love you, sweetie," in her half-asleep state. I would squeeze her hand back. In her delirium, I think she thought I was her daughter. It was the least I could do to repay her.

Two days later, Ms. D. died quietly in her sleep. Gary, the team senior, gave the daughter the news when she came in to see her mother, and I asked if I could come with him, since I had spent so much time with Ms. D. As Gary talked to Ms. D.'s daughter, I looked over to Ms. D.'s resting body. So calm now. Ms. D.'s daughter's tears came pouring out. "I didn't expect she would go so soon. She was a good mom. I loved her, and I'm glad that we chose not to impose any extra suffering on her."

"Yes, you made the right decision," Gary said.

I wonder what she would have thought, had she been able to talk to her mom again, or had she been there that first night after her mom was admitted. I looked at her, and as I left, I held her hand and stifled the tears before they could come out. At least I knew now that Ms. D. had a daughter who really cared. But I felt so guilty. Guilty for having let Dave continue with the sticks, for not speaking out at least. But Dave, being a genuinely good guy, felt it too.

As doctors, we make decisions on the fly, sometimes with little time to think. We make these choices, and we can only hope that they are for the best. But if I have learned anything from this experience, it is the fallibility of a physician's desire to "better." That wish is what makes a physician's spirit so special; that determined nature to help is our weakness as well. By the time we wake up from our miracle-mission coma, three needle sticks later, a helpless old woman is at her deathbed, wailing for mercy.

I'm sorry, Ms. D. I needed to say sorry to you.

Coney Island

Yana Pikman

For the first time during that week, I was told about the patient's story before entering the room and reading her chart. "This is a young woman with metastatic cervical cancer, which is impinging on her ureter. We will place a stent to keep it open," the attending told me. My heart sank. I had been living in a world where cervical cancer is detected early by Pap smears and was shocked to see this woman squeezed into the operating-room schedule between a TURP (transurethral resection of the prostate) and cystoscopy cases. Did the medical system fail this person?

When we walked into the room, the patient was already on the operating table. I expected her to be distraught but found a smiling, calm, and very warm woman. She had a rosary and a religious pendant pressed tight against her chest. We chatted about her kids, three and five years old, living in Florida after having grown up in New York, and her most recent procedure to remove several abdominal masses. We talked about Brooklyn and discovered that we were both from Coney Island. She had moved to Florida to be with her husband; I was considering the possibility of moving across country for my love. I could see myself in her: immigrant, growing up in the same place, similar goals of living the American dream. But the idea of her cancer could not leave my mind. As she was dreaming, eating, laughing, her cancer was feeding itself, decreasing her chances of seeing her kids grow up with the same dreams. I wanted to ask her how she could be so strong and composed, smiling and making jokes.

We started the procedure. We intubated her, and the urologist went in with his scope and injected dye into the urinary system. She had a bifurcated, or branching, ureter on the side of the compression. People really had that! I was amazed by the stent placement, the images of the ureters, the serial fluoroscopy views for visualizing the constriction, stent placement, and filling of the ureter afterward. I was amazed by the technique, the visual stimuli.

But afterward I felt guilty for not thinking about her throughout. It was a strange juxtaposition, the surgery and the personal story. The most interesting cases are often the most devastating for the patient. My scientific interest and patient experience had originally attracted me to the field of medicine, but now, after talking to her, I felt guilty looking inside her with a scope. I felt as if I had invaded her, and after having connected to her, I felt almost invaded myself.

Later in the evening, I went with another student to do a post-op check on her. Again we chatted about her sister, who had come up from New York to be with her in the hospital, and about her husband's struggle with keeping up the household in her absence. The other student interrupted us to ask about pain, gas, and bowel movements. He wrote down her answers carefully, making sure to cover all the necessary surgical points. I did not want to know about her bowel movements. I was really enjoying chatting with her and wanted to try to make her feel comfortable in the cold hospital, so far away from her family.

But I was not doing my job. I had an assignment to do a post-op check, and yet my colleague seemed the only one focused on that goal. I wondered what would have happened if I were alone. Would I have been able to do my job in a case where I related so closely to the patient? Was it too dangerous to be emotionally connected to the patient? But at the same time I had little control over the situation. When the other student was done filling out the form, he sent me that eye signal that means "We have somewhere else to be," and after doing a quick physical exam, we left the room.

"Cervical cancer is a sexually transmitted disease," the student told me after we walked out. True. But I felt as if I had been slapped in the face. I was offended. He was saying that it was her fault, and I wanted to defend her. But did he mean it that way? I could not handle the objective, scientific fact. I had taken to her, and the facts were too painful. If it was up to me to do a procedure on her at that point, I don't think I would have been able to do it. How was it possible to try to connect with a patient, to try to understand what she was going through, but at the same time to remain able to perform the necessary job?

I felt powerless against any sort of disease process and found myself wondering how the medical profession even works. Combining the mechanism of disease with the personal experience of disease and the fight against it, on the part of both the patient, their loved ones, and the physician, seemed to be an issue greater than life itself. We were on the side of treatment, fighting against the invading tumor. Her kids were at home, waiting for their mother to return. Where was the disease? I guess this is why the patient needs to be treated as a whole, but in her case I could not consolidate all of those parts. She was a person whom I connected with closely, someone I would have talked with extensively if we had met at a bar. I had looked inside her with a scope. I could not effectively do a post-op check, and when I heard a poorly expressed statement about her disease, it sent a pain to my core.

Given another chance, I would still have talked to her as I did and probably would have connected just as much. I do not want to become a doctor who does not know her patients. But how do you provide good care when you cannot remain productive and objective? Perhaps that is where the medical team comes in, with different parts of the team serving different parts of the person. I tried to think of how I would want my doctor to act and which questions I would want to hear two hours after my surgery. I wanted to be asked about my pain, though perhaps not about my bowel movements; I would also want someone to care enough to ask about my visitor or the pictures on my nightstand. But I wonder if all of these types of caring can be combined in a single person. Perhaps that consolidation is something I can learn on the wards.

The Naked Truth

Joseph Corkery

THE COMMON MIND-SET among most college-aged men was that pretty much every scenario involving a naked woman was exciting. I remember wondering, somewhat anxiously, before the first few days of medical school, how this experience would necessarily change in the clinical setting. I frequently found myself contemplating how I (not to mention my then girlfriend) would react to the frequently intimate examinations of members of the opposite sex.

Our class's first encounter with clinical nudity was in the anatomy lab. In general, the formaldehyde stench of death and the dangerously clumsy manipulation of our scalpels greatly overwhelmed any of our concerns about modesty. I remember a significant classwide loss of modesty as people began to casually change into and out of their scrubs in the hallways. In many ways, the anatomy course served as a dual rite of passage, accustoming us not only to death but to the unemotional clinical view of the human body. Within a few short weeks, we grew accustomed to viewing the naked body in a completely detached way.

It was not long after this that we learned to cast aside (without being intoxicated) our fears of and judgments about discussing sex with relative strangers. Within months, a medical history that included sexual questions such as "Do you prefer men, women, or both?" ceased to be taboo. By the end of first year, I felt reasonably confident that while wrapped in the protective garb of my white coat, I was ready to comfortably, appropriately, and with a straight face discuss sexual practices with any of the Victoria's Secret models.

In our first year, we had mastered seeing and talking, but something even more personal remained: touching. Most of our second year was dedicated to learning how to touch a patient and how to accomplish this in the most comfortable manner for both parties. With extensive practice and the amazing generosity of my patients, I learned how to touch patients in a way that allowed me to acquire clinical information without creating an uncomfortable or inappropriate situation.

With all this experience under my belt, I felt ready to begin the "undressed" rehearsal that is the third year of medical school. I was surprised at how easy it was to interact with patients clothed only in hospital gowns. There was something strangely unique about the entire situation that made sexy lingerie strewn over a chair surprisingly normal and not out of the ordinary. Perhaps my experience was tempered by the fact that I am married and could more easily distance myself from these otherwise bizarre situations. And I noticed patients eyeing the gold ring circling my fourth finger and wondered if that might ease the situation for them. Of course, I didn't like what that interpretation implied about possible patient perceptions of unmarried physicians, but as a result, I did find myself making sure my left hand was easily visible.

As my surgery rotation progressed, I was pleased at how it was becoming easy to view all patients in a completely asexual manner. Sadly I was not prepared for the coming experience that would shatter my "clinical goggles."

It was another ordinary day on my plastics elective during my surgical clerkship. I reported bright and early to the operating room for a breast augmentation case. I was definitely somewhat uncomfortable helping out with cosmetic surgery but felt some comfort in that this was a redo of a post-cancer reconstruction. As I entered the OR, I found the patient lying naked and prepped on the operating table. Her breasts were exposed and soon the focus of the group's attention. One of her implants had leaked, and now there was a mass of crumpled plastic where a smooth surface was supposed to be. The surgeons took turns examining this breast to learn the results of a failed augmentation.

The procedure went smoothly from first incision to insertion of the new implants. However, before closing the incision, the surgeons had to adjust the size of the new implants. Implants are adjusted by increasing or decreasing the amount of saline in them. To get the adjustments correct, the operating table was raised into a reclining position so that the patient (still under anesthesia) would be sitting upright. At this point, the attending, the resident, the scrub nurse, the circulator, and I found ourselves all eyeing the patient from the foot of the table, trying to decide which side was bigger. There seemed to be no good consensus, particularly because nobody could agree upon whose left we were talking about. The dispute was resolved by the resident, who cupped both breasts simultaneously and assessed their symmetry. Multiple iterations of this process occurred before the decision to close was made. I found myself surrounded by, and being drawn into, discussions of which sizings looked best and were the most visually appealing. Then someone jokingly suggested inviting the husband into the room to find out what appealed to him the most. I remember the resident expressing confusion that the patient requested not to have them significantly enlarged, only to be rebuffed by the scrub nurse with the comment, "She doesn't want to have to buy a whole new wardrobe after this."

It was at this point that I realized that somehow we had all lost our clinical mind-set in the examination of this woman. This was a discomforting realization, but at the same time, it seemed almost a necessity if the surgeon was to accomplish his task with the perfection to which most surgeons aspire. I see now that the ongoing challenge will be to accomplish the surgical objectives without losing respect for the patients' bodies.

Losing Your Mind

Esther Huang

The brain is the only organ that is aware of its own dysfunction.
—My attending

"I'M SUCH A DUMB-DUMB." The words seemed strange coming from the lips of an attractive elderly woman poised in bed with an aristocratic air and Pilates-perfect posture. Strange, but perhaps not unexpected, given that she had just been unable to spell *world* backward, subtract three from ninety-six, or recall the current month of the year. It was sadly striking to see her mind come so close ("Who was the president before Bush?" "Mr. . . . Cool . . ."), to hear her frustration ("Oh, I used to know!").

"We understand this isn't you," the intern told her, "that this is something put upon you—we all know. You shouldn't blame yourself."

With an imploring smile, she asked, "Would you please tell everyone else that too?"

This woman had no warning of the fungus that spread to her brain, and could have done little to prevent it. The condition was so rare that none of her previous physicians had seen it before.

She would look over at her husband and ask, "Am I doing OK?" during the history taking. "You're doing fine, sweetheart," he'd say every time in his low and resonant tones. When she grew forgetful or weary, he'd fill in the rest. When he recounted poignant events, his voice would break down. He refused to let her go to the bathroom by herself, to the point of inconvenience; he didn't want her to see how she looked in the mirror after her craniotomy—half her hair shaved, bruising around her eyes from the surgery—not when she'd always been sensitive about her appearance. Perhaps some things in which we stake our identities last longer than others. Or perhaps the loss of one makes another stand out in bolder, more beautiful relief. Perhaps in the end, the identities that last aren't found in anything we possess at all—skills, objects, appearances, even our minds—but in the relationships we cultivate, with our loved ones and perhaps with our God. It's good to be reminded of these things: because cultivation takes intentionality, investment, sacrifice, and some deal of courage. Courage to love and receive love. Courage to be entrusted with vulnerabilities and to reveal our own. Courage to value the journeys we make together. It's good to be reminded, because the voice telling me to heed these things more is not the blaring one signaling an upcoming exam or a call night, nor the sirenlike lure of prestige; it is that quiet, still voice inside, ready to speak if I'm willing to listen. When I decide what to invest my identity in, what to value most in life, what to have faith in, here's hoping I tune in to that one. Here's hoping I remember the woman who lost her mind, only to find herself more loved by the one beside her.

Breathing, the Movie

Joe Wright

Long before I decided to go to medical school, I wanted to become a film director. In college, I took classes in film and video production and analysis and history. Friends often asked me whether those classes ruined movies for me; they thought that knowing the mechanisms of moviemaking would spoil the experience of escaping into the world of the film.

I knew what they meant. But I never found that I enjoyed movies less. In fact, during that time in my life I usually saw at least two movies in the theater each week. Often I would walk to a nearby movie theater and just see whatever was playing next, whether it was a B-grade Hollywood cop movie or a slow, ponderous European film. A nice shot of a city, a clever twist in a genre formula, or an adventurous use of sound—all might excite me even in the midst of a totally insufferable film.

Probably any rigorous training changes the way you see the world. In the Vipassana Buddhist meditation tradition, as in many other meditative practices, one tries to simply focus on the physical fact of breathing fully in and out, as a way of living in the present. Before medical school, I took a class that taught this kind of meditation. As we sat and our minds inevitably wandered, our teacher would softly say, "Return to your breathing," meaning to return to simply feeling your breathing moving your body as a constant, gentle physical fact. After that class, I thought about breathing in a new way: as a kind of center of daily experience, a source of calm.

Now, becoming a doctor, I also think about breathing as pushes and pulls of tissues and muscles and fluids, full of nuance. Not just air moving in and out, but the complex mechanics that move it, and the structure of the hemoglobin in a red blood cell picking up oxygen, and more than that too. And this is a new kind of awareness. It is like what I once knew about films, thinking, How'd they do that dolly shot? or Nice L-cut. I am aware not only of the breath but also of how it is made.

Just as in my film student days, it's not that I always understand it. In fact, at least as often, I eventually realize that I've got another part of it wrong again, and I have to go back and relearn it. Medical school makes me see breathing differently not only because of my new understanding, but even more, because I know there are huge worlds of things to be understood, ever-finer levels of detail to struggle with and then, finally, to know.

And so my friend's little boy is sitting on my lap, listening to a story I'm reading him, and I feel his body moving with his breathing. Giving my friend a hug good-bye, I feel the movement of air moving in and her chest and belly pushing out, then falling back as air moves out. Ribs expanding and pulling the lungs out with them, and then the lung tissue pulling back. And in moments like this, I feel it or see it in someone else, and think about it for a second, and breathing becomes one of those sudden short moments where the filmmakers have done something beautiful and clever and I think, That's genius, and I think, I love this movie.

Donor

Kimberly Layne Collins

You stared through the white cloth into
the other side, while your body lay
exposed on the table before us.

You, our teacher, our first patient,
would not complain through our probing
or criticize when we cut too deep

or in the wrong direction.
As we opened your chest and looked
into ourselves, what we saw mirrored

what we all feel inside but could not know
until you showed us: how fragile is our flesh,
which gives so easily beneath the scalpel:

how thin the boundary between self and world.
I knew you'd been under the knife before—
the gray scar marking where your right breast hung.

I wonder how that must have felt. I know how
your lungs sit in the recesses of your thoracic cavity
and how your bowels twist through your abdomen

because I have pulled and cut and lifted them out.
I have sliced through the muscle of your heart.
What kept it beating so many years?

Who did you love? Who loved you?
How strange it was to be able to reach inside you
when you could not reach back,

your nimble fingers stiffened into place by rigor mortis;
to pull at your limbs, without asking permission,
in order to crack your ribs;

to saw through your skull and lift out
the center of your thoughts, without knowing
what last ones still lingered.

Living with Mrs. Longwood

Rajesh G. Shah

Even before you start medical school, there's this feeling—this unwritten rule passed down from practitioner to student—that your first patient will always be a part of you, that he or she will touch your soul in a way you didn't know possible. No matter the condition or problem the patient has—even an ingrown toenail would count—that patient will always be a part of your birth as a healer.

I knew this; I even expected it, with a certain logical fallacy that this patient was merely the first of a long line I would treat in my lifelong education as a conjurer of the medical arts. I knew this with all certainty, and therefore a part of me even wanted to challenge such a stereotypical notion of attachment and prove the entire medical establishment wrong. But I'll be damned if the medical Gods didn't conspire to teach me otherwise and to show me the exact reason *why* all doctors remember their first patient so well, and *why* they always cherish that memory with a certain familiar fondness.

Let me tell you about my first patient, Mrs. Longwood.

The first mention of her name came to me with the sort of wry medical wit that invariably becomes necessary to pass days filled with unending hours and ever-demanding illnesses. No disrespect is meant to the patient, and certainly you'd be hard pressed to prove otherwise, but still there is an unsaid bit of communication that becomes obvious when your resident says to you with a huge grin on her face, "Why don't you go take care of the patient in room eleven of the ER? This will be a *nice* and *easy* one for you."

So I did. I was expecting a hard case, but I certainly didn't expect a simple, blank stare and nonsensical guttural sounds when I asked her name and why she was here. I paused for a minute and was dreaming up new and interesting ways of primal communication when her son entered with a fresh cup of coffee. I felt relieved to see him, knowing that my job would be easier, but this feeling was soon washed away by the obvious realization that someone who could not even communicate with me was very, very sick.

They transferred Mrs. Longwood up to an inpatient floor fairly quickly, and I pulled her son into an empty conference room to get a history as best I could. It turned out that Mrs. Longwood had a bulging right knee filled with a corrosive osteosarcoma that was slowly progressing. The pain from this was unimaginable, and as the pain became worse, the long-term facility in which she resided had increased her transdermal fentanyl patch. But they had done so too quickly in the past couple of days, and she had become delirious and had begun to speak in nonsensical words and point toward visual hallucinations of her adolescent children, who had long since become middle-aged. It seemed simple enough: reduce the pain medication back to her previous baseline, and wait until she regained her cognitive abilities. And for the most part, it was just that simple—at least until we began to address her other major problems, like the cancerous mass growing in her knee.

The first three days were unremarkable, as she slowly but steadily flushed the fentanyl from her system and regained her mental faculties. As this happened, though, little personality quirks came to the surface. For one, she had a severe anxiety problem. She had taken Valium several times daily for at least the past twenty years and requested what she liked to call her "happy pills" whenever I asked about her pain. This was not a problem, mind you, as we could not safely withdraw them anyway, with the danger of a withdrawal-induced seizure. Besides, since she'd taken them every day for twenty years, to withdraw them now would have been downright cruel.

I must admit that I felt a certain resentment toward her. In my mind, all anxiety problems were nothing more than a discreet way to obtain recreational drugs—a socially acceptable way to get "mother's little helper" for those times when one needed to relax. It had never occurred to me that some people live with an anxiety so severe that they cannot contain it.

The irony is overwhelming—that I, someone who takes pain medication daily to deal with chronic pain from meningitis, and who *constantly* chastises the medical system for its fearful inhibition about prescribing pain medication to those who complain of pain, would categorize all anxiety patients as liars and socially acceptable drug abusers. But thus is the nature of prejudice: we take only those examples that validate our preconceived notions and discard any examples to the contrary. And in doing so, we prove to ourselves time and time again that our beliefs *must* be correct.

But in treating Mrs. Longwood on the third day, a miraculous event occurred. She asked for her "happy pills" as usual, and I ordered 0.5 mg of Ativan. Almost instantaneously, as the nurse pushed the intravenous drug into her veins, she was transformed from a blathering fool filled with nonsensical half sentences into a lucid, well-mannered, kind old lady who told enchanting tales of days gone by and carried on normal conversations just as the rest of us did.

Now, I had always been taught that "benzos" *inhibited* neural activity by raising levels of a neurotransmitter referred to as GABA (gamma-aminobutyric acid) and as such would make the patient *less* capable and even euphoric. With a sense of wonder, I ran to my resident and described my encounter with this obvious paradox of medical science.

"Raj, have you ever been really anxious and worried, so much so that you can't think straight and are filled with all these unwanted thoughts? That's how she feels every day because of her anxiety, and even more so by being in this strange, scary environment. When you gave her the Ativan, you helped her get rid of the anxiety and unwanted thoughts and to finally be herself. That's why she's so clearheaded now."

It amazed me that all my years of preconceived belief were wrong—that here before my eyes was living proof that anxiety was indeed a real, inhibiting condition that caused actual medical problems that interfered with normal lives, and not merely the textbook justification for drug companies to make commercials featuring happy people running through butterfly-filled fields of daisies so that the companies could make outrageous sums of money. Here, before my eyes, was Mrs. Longwood.

I began to spend a great deal of time with her after this, so much so that I would check in on her almost every hour and use my free time to make sure she was OK. This mostly consisted of little things like getting her water, as the medications made her incredibly parched, and checking her pain levels and asking the nurse to give her more morphine when needed. But for the most part, I just enjoyed getting to know her family and listening to stories about Boston in the old days—a Boston that now exists only in history books.

Because of her anxiety, she often accused the nurses of neglecting her and making false statements, so they rarely ventured into her room unless absolutely needed. This didn't bother me, though, because it just gave me more to do for her.

Over time, however, Mrs. Longwood began to think of me as *her* doctor, although I explained to her each time that I was only a medical student and that my name was Raj, not Ron. But eventually I began to enjoy being seen as a doctor—even though I had little real power over her care—and no longer minded when she called me Dr. Ron. She began to expect me to be with her, and I enjoyed being there.

But one day the cancer and radiation teams converged on her room with her family to explain that she needed to have her leg amputated in order to save her life. She began to cry. After all, who among us wouldn't cry if we were to lose a limb, especially at her age, since it meant that she would never walk again? As her thoughts cleared, she refused the surgery and to lose her limb, despite discussions with her doctors and with her sons and husband.

I read every article I could find on osteosarcoma and paged all the members of her team to ask about alternatives, until the sad day came when I realized there were no alternatives. Radiation and chemo had been tried and ultimately made no difference. Her leg had to be amputated, and there was *nothing* else that could be done, not in the power of a medical student, and not in the power of a physician.

Her family sat with her one last time to convince her of its necessity, but she was a stubborn woman and refused. After her family left, on the last day the surgical team would take the case, I sat alone with her and explained the necessity of the procedure. I didn't want to see her die of cancer. She was too wonderful a person for the world to lose, but more important, she was *my* patient. Others could ask for her consent and accept defeat, but

I was Dr. Ron—*her* doctor. I sat with her on her bedside, held her hand, and asked her one last time about the surgery to save her life. She wept softly as we spoke, and I wiped her tears with my hand as she asked if anything else could be done. I told her with as much composure as I could muster that as far as I knew, from my reading and from speaking with others, nothing else could be done.

She looked at me. "I know you would never lie to me, Dr. Ron. You're a wonderful person. God bless you."

In Indian culture, the blessings of one's elders are worth more than all the material success in the world and are in a sense a blessing from God. Elders are cherished and honored as the wisest, and it is the honor of sons or daughters to take care of their parents as they age and become less capable. Nursing homes do not exist in India—because no son or daughter would ever lose the honor of caring for his or her elders, especially a parent.

Here, as I sat with Mrs. Longwood, as she wept into my hands, I had received the blessings of my elders—the greatest gift I could possibly receive. In the morning, with her family surrounding her to steady her hands as she wrote, she signed the consent form for the surgery she needed to save her life. It was performed two days later without complications, and although she suffered greatly from the pain of a new wound, she was alive.

Her wounds eventually healed and she went back to the long-term-care facility where she normally stayed, but Mrs. Longwood is still with me. I think about her often, especially when I see an older patient, and I know that in these people lie the cherished memories of a life worth living—a life that history will record from a unique perspective that nobody else could have contributed in quite the same way.

I have begun my medical training—my indoctrination into a life of learning and of service—and I wonder how many more Mrs. Longwoods I will see.

III.

Easing Suffering and Loss

The first question which the priest and the Levite asked was: "If I stop to help this man, what will happen to me?" But . . . the good Samaritan reversed the question: "If I do not stop to help this man, what will happen to him?"

MARTIN LUTHER KING JR.

Not Since 1918

Kedar Mate

M R. BEACON IS SIXTY-EIGHT. I don't know him
well; in fact, before tonight I couldn't really have claimed to
know him at all. So unfortunately I can't provide the gloriously
succinct history of present illness that you've no doubt come to
expect within the first few lines of anything written. Indeed,
despite the fact that I have recently begun to seek out the "chief
complaints" of all of my new acquaintances, I cannot claim to
know much about Mr. Beacon's.

No, Mr. Beacon, to me, was just a guy lying beyond two doors
in a positive-pressure isolation room on the fourteenth floor of
the hospital. He has, like many on the dreaded "Hiroshima"
floor, leukemia of the adult variety: acute myelogenous leukemia
(AML). All I knew about Mr. Beacon before tonight was that
he had experienced some mental-status changes on my previous
on-call night. When I'd gone to see him then, I'd found him

lethargic, though awake and oriented, times an unfortunate two. I never pay much attention to "AAO x 2," because I frequently forget where I am and what the date is, but in Mr. Beacon's case, he'd forgotten his name. This earned him a neurology consult, and when the reflex-hammer jockeys (as my intern called them) emerged from the air lock all surgically capped and gowned and talking about pontine hemorrhage, we got worried. I quickly fled to the nearest computer before any questions regarding neurology were asked of me. My Internet Oracle informed me that said pontine hemorrhage was, indeed, a thing to be feared. Turned out that after much imaging, Mr. Beacon didn't really have a pontine hemorrhage after all, just a "region of focal hypodensity" that didn't amount to much. In the morning, much to our delight, he regained his sense of self.

That would have been the first and only time I met Mr. Beacon, except that last night, the Red Sox were playing the Oakland A's in game five of the American League Championship Series. It was an unbelievable game, coming down to the age-old Little Leaguer's mythical moment: bottom of the ninth, bases loaded, two men out, full count, and *you're* on the mound. And so it was last night, when sometime after midnight Derek Lowe, one of Boston's finest pitchers, threw a sizzling strike that ended the game and sent half of the fourteenth floor into arrhythmias.

Last night, Hiroshima, not to be crass, was on fire. Every ten to fifteen minutes, cursing and screaming would erupt from several rooms at once, sending the nurses scurrying to check for possible codes, falls, sudden oxygen desaturations, or any one of an assortment of tragedies that may befall the hospitalized on a given evening.

I, for one, was paying extra-special attention to my three patients, all of whom were eagerly watching the ball game, regardless of how much they cared about baseball. One of my new guys, Mr. Storrow, is a soft-spoken young man with unresectable pancreatic cancer who's got a wife and two boys, ages ten and twelve. His bowel was obstructed from the cancer mass, he felt nauseated, and he'd been vomiting every half hour to hour, but somehow he managed to stay riveted to the game, updating me on each pitcher's pitch count every time I'd stop by. Mr. Vernon was watching the game over his hot-rod magazines. He likes to build cars, he'd told me earlier in the day. On one of my visits every fifteen minutes to check on his falling blood pressure and Pedro Martinez's strikeout count, he offered to explain how to fix my muffler if the Sox won the game. Mr. Joyce, my last patient this evening, is a great old guy with lower extremity lymphedema from inguinal radiation therapy, which has now developed a cellulitis. Baseball's not really his thing, but when you're watching baseball with Mr. J., or anyone else who's lived in Boston long enough, you feel like you're sitting in Fenway Park in the 1940s with Ted Williams stepping to the plate.

While my beloved patients were relatively peaceful in their adoration for the famous Boston Red Sox, behind two airtight doors Mr. Beacon's room was all kinds of chaos—ground zero for Red Sox fandom in Hiroshima. With every pitch erupted a chorus of expletives and cheers, better described as a collection of yips and yelps, emitted from a mucositic throat three times sub-jected to induction chemotherapy. A favorite refrain echoed out from beyond the doors: "Sit down, ya li'l pissah!" I was drawn to his room like a sixth inning fastball to Manny Ramirez's bat.

Inside I found Mr. Beacon, propped up, wasted, his neck scaly, contracted, his tongue lounging at the corners of his drooping mouth. Eyes unmovable, affixed to the television set that hung from the ceiling. Had I tried to check his extraocular move-ments just then, he might have tried to do bodily harm to me. Accompanying Mr. Beacon was his wife of forty-three years and his son of thirty-five years, both fully dressed—beneath their yellow neutropenic precautionary gowns—in the fall line of Red Sox memorabilia. On their heads, as on Mr. Beacon's head, sat Red Sox caps with blue surgical crowns. When I walked in and introduced myself, explaining that I couldn't keep myself away from this boisterous inner sanctum of Boston baseball fans, Mr. Beacon's wife quietly handed me a hat and told me to start pray-ing. There we were, four loonies, awake and oriented to only one thing: the flickering TV that hung from the ceiling.

By the bottom of the ninth inning, the score was Boston 4, Oakland 3. Oakland's batters were coming to bat, and when the first two Oakland batters were walked on base, Mr. Beacon was huffing and puffing, no longer able to communicate to us his lifelong frustration with the failure of the Red Sox. Any other moment, his hyperventilating might have caused some alarm; his oxygen saturation, which I quietly checked, was hovering between ninety-two and ninety-four—lower than it should be. When the Sox went to the bull pen, I asked him how he was feeling.

"Like hell," came the gravelly reply, his eyes more alive than they'd been the last time I'd seen them. Confident he meant the game, we all turned back to it. Wife, son, and med student were now huddled around Mr. Beacon, hands clasped in some pagan ritual. . . . Two outs came swiftly, and life came to a standstill . . . all of our hearts pounding. Mr. Beacon's monitor was showing some premature ventricular contractions—we ignored them. Two balls, one strike, one foul ball, and then Derek Lowe delivered the two-two pitch. We froze, Mr. Beacon held his breath, causing his O$_2$ sat to dip past ninety to eighty-six, the monitor beeped loudly, and I had an undetected myocardial infarction . . . "STRIKE THREE," came the call! The game was over; the Red Sox had won. We rejoiced.

Mr. Beacon's sixty-eight years old, he's got AML, and he's been through several rounds of chemotherapy, relapsing consistently after each one. He's on comfort measures only now. And most of the docs I've heard chatting about him wouldn't give him much of a shot at seeing the Red Sox return next year to the American League Championship Series. I guess this makes me sad, but today, one day after that miraculous victory, I feel happy that Mr. Beacon could see that. Last night must have felt like living once again to Mr. Beacon. It certainly made me feel like I was living, and it made his family feel alive too. About a half hour after the victory, I stopped by to continue the postgame revelry.

"Not since 1918," Mr. Beacon said, reflecting on the Red Sox's last World Series win. "I hope I can hang on to watch them do it again."

The Tortoise and the Air

Vesna Ivančić

CHAPTER ONE: FRESH AIR

This is the story of an old man who felt like a tortoise, or rather the back of a tortoise. Only it was his front that felt this way. His scarred, bloated, rock-hard belly felt exactly as I, an inexperienced percussionist, imagined a tortoiseshell would feel if you were to attempt percussing it. The analogy seemed no more unusual to me at the time than anything else I'd thought since entering the world of hospitals the week before. As medical students, we percuss all kinds of things and, to the great dismay of our clinical professors, extract just about as much information from the endeavor as you would if you attempted percussing a turtle. Besides, I'd been thinking about turtles lately.

Just that morning I had reluctantly taken the turtle off my necklace for the first time. It had been three months since we'd broken up—a breakup that was just as unexpected as the gift of the turtle on our trip to Phoenix the previous Thanksgiving. Three months apart after three years together, and I was starting a whole new life that week. It was obvious: the turtle had to go. I was a big fan of symbolism. I wasn't superstitious; I just liked making connections. And so I unclasped the chain, and a shiny brown turtle swam jerkily down, landing tailfirst on a bookshelf. I sighed, realizing it was one of the bookshelves that he had put up in my room. What was the half-life, I wondered, for removing all traces of him from my system? Was I simply being romantic, or were such thoughts pathetic by now? I couldn't decide, and either way, the turtle's day had come.

Chapter Two: Wasted Air

An hour later, we were dutifully rounding on the list of patients assigned to the Red team. Most of our time was spent hunting for signs of infection. We scoured records of vital signs for fever, flashed light at wounds from every angle, and attempted to express purulence, otherwise known as squeezing to see if pus comes out. Then, of course, we'd reevaluate the appropriateness of antibiotic armaments assigned to each patient and coax them into admitting recent flatus or bowel movements. A positive answer relieved and delighted us, even at six in the morning, and we'd march off like a troop of white elephants through a sleepy jungle to the next room.

I don't remember the first time we rounded on Mr. U. What first made him memorable to me was the day he set a trap for the herd of general surgeons stomping through the halls of the White and Ellison buildings. We were going along at our usual clip, en route, inexorably, to salvation: the operating room. I glanced at my watch—7:27. Not much longer now, I thought, until we will be scrubbed in, under the lights, over a prepped patient, beside the Mayo tray, and ready to do a satisfying colectomy. Mr. U. had a different morning in mind for us, and it all began when he politely refused his nasogastric tube.

It was my first week on a surgical clerkship, and I had already been taught that the NG tube, which sucked air and fluids out of the stomach, up through the esophagus, and out the nose, was, oddly enough, the exact way we treat people whose stomachs are as hugely distended and full of air as Mr. U.'s was. Apparently Mr. U. knew this as well. He'd had an NG tube before, and "No way, you can't make me; I won't have it," was his response to a second encounter. My first reaction was in keeping with that of the other members of my team: nothing short of exasperation. I had never seen anyone who needed an NG tube more. OK, so I had only seen a few people who needed an NG tube at all. But the guy's tympanitic! I thought to myself—a word, not to mention an argument, I had never heard of one week before. Never mind that: it was obvious even to a layman that Mr. U.'s abdomen was all blown up and rock hard—turtle hard—or, as we medical students like to proclaim, this was definitely badness. Worse yet, his ostomy was kinked in exactly such a way that the distension was pushing his folded-up intestine against the wall of his abdomen, where it had no hope of uncoiling. His obstruction was getting worse. He needed desperately to be decompressed. In other words, the air had to come out of him.

And yet the only air that came out of anyone was the wasted breath of my senior surgical resident as he attempted to obtain Mr. U.'s consent for "snaking down the tube." I especially noted the "Come on, let's do this, we're all on the same team" tactic—partly because it seemed, at first, to be working, and partly because, let's face it, we may all be on the same team, but I sure as hell would rather be on the shove-it-in side of the NG tube. After what felt like an hour but was probably five minutes, my frustrated resident and intern left the room mumbling, somewhat rhetorically, "Why do these people come to hospitals if they don't want to be treated?"

I stood there, confused, aware of the patient's presence, aware of my team's absence, upset by the conflict, seeing merit on both sides, and unsure of what to do next. In the months to come, I would realize that the way I felt at that moment was to become my usual state of being as a medical student. At the time, though, I was still naïve and optimistic. I decided to try something that hadn't been tried—the one thing even I, as a medical student, knew how to do as well as anyone else. I begged. I pleaded with him to let them put in the tube. I honestly trusted these people and fervently believed it was in Mr. U.'s best interest to have the NG tube if they said so. He, of course, said no to all my pleas. And just as suddenly as when you're staring at one of those pictures that all your friends claim is actually a three-dimensional hologram, and all you can see is blue and gray sparkles until, abruptly and without transition, the other picture pops out at you, Mr. U.'s perspective popped out at me. Suddenly I believed he was perfectly right in refusing the NG tube. There were no guarantees it would solve all his problems. He had every right to refuse treatment. Besides, he swore he got this way all the time at home and was always fine by morning. Why should he believe this situation to be different? He didn't feel any pain. "If there was something bad going on, I would know it," he said over and over.

I didn't even want to argue that point. How could I? There are some things you just know you're going to get through, even though they may seem like a big deal to someone else. For example, you're running with your boyfriend, and the cramps just get too horrible, and your head is exploding even after two extra-strength Tylenol, and you've been bleeding for thirty hours by then, so you just have to stop running. But you know you're going to be OK, and you'll be OK a month later too, when it happens all over again. So you laugh at him as he promises to desist from calling 911 and shakes his head with that worried, apologetic, guilty look in his eyes, as if his being a male had been a choice.

"Please, don't ask me again, dear," Mr. U. rasped through the oxygen mask. I felt like Luke Skywalker talking to the dying Darth Vader. Only I wasn't related to Mr. U. at all; we'd only met days ago, and even then, he was introduced to me as COPD.

Chapter Three: Trapped Air

That week, Mr. U. had become for me the personification of flow-volume loops. I'd only seen pictures of them in textbooks and on PowerPoint slides and, if our teacher was old fashioned, in real-time chalk. Flow-volume loops are complex graphs that describe a patient's breathing pattern. I remembered thinking how ironic and unfortunate it was that patients viewed their chronic obstructive pulmonary disease as one that makes them unable to get enough air in, and that doctors viewed it as a disease that makes lungs unable to get enough air out. So how do we treat the trapped air? Mr. U. had little tubes up each nostril giving him even more air—five times as much oxygen, in fact, as the rest of us breathe. I couldn't figure out if air was his enemy or his friend.

Chapter Four: Free Air

A couple of days later, the answer was obvious. His X-ray revealed one of the few things I could recognize: a thin black moon of air lifting up a stretch of white diaphragm. Free air in his belly, while worrisome, was also exciting because it meant we were going straight where I wanted to be: the operating room.

The question was, did Mr. U. want to be there? His choices weren't presented with the gravity and melodrama that I had grown to expect from movies. There was no dimming of lights, no music in the background. It wasn't even raining outside. Wasn't it always supposed to rain? Thomas Hardy would have arranged for a downpour. I wondered if this was only the dress rehearsal for the real moment when we'd tell him.

Surgery: they weren't sure he would survive it, but they were sure he would die without it. To me the choice seemed to be, did he want to die tonight or in a couple of weeks? Now or later? But that's not what he was asked. He was asked if he would approve the preparing of the operating room. He was asked if they had his permission to call the anesthesiologist in case her services became necessary. He was asked if he was ready for the transport team to come up. Mr. U. was not stupid. He could see all these events were corollaries to the real decision. Selfish questions doctors ask when we're trying to decide what we have to do next: Did he need a CT scan? Should we call for the anesthesia consult? Was his consent signed? From Mr. U.'s point of view, though, the big question was still, surgery, and risk dying tonight, or no surgery, and risk dying next week or month? Die tonight or later? His answer was always the same: "I don't know yet. I'm waiting for my brother to come before I decide."

Chapter Five: Airhead

The guy who came looked like a punk high school kid.

"I'm here from transport to take you to the OR," he declared in that couldn't-care-less voice all teenage boys master.

The doctors had all left the room by then, and for once, so had the nurses. The only one remaining was Mr. U. He looked so small and helpless to me—a tiny turtle with big blue eyes, a tuft of white hair slicked back like Pat Riley's, and an oxygen mask. I sat down in the only chair, with all my youth and health and all the fierce protectiveness I usually reserve for my little sister. Only now I was going to protect Mr. U. from the boogeyman, currently disguised as the punk high school kid with the stretcher.

"He isn't going anywhere yet," I told Mr. Gum-Chewing, Tattooed Stretcher Pusher. "He's waiting for his brother to come."

The kid puffed, annoyed with us both, and snapped his gloves off noisily before turning around. Mr. U.'s eyes were livid.

"I already told them that," he reminded me. "What's wrong with these people?"

What could I say? I knew the feeling. It was that Alice-in-Wonderland terror that comes over you when you can't recognize the social rules of the game and you think that either everyone around you is insane or you are, and it's much easier to believe and harder to swallow that it's only you. I've felt that way throughout much of medical school.

With the stretcher gone, Mr. U. calmed down a little, and we resumed waiting for his brother. My job became that of a scout: every few minutes he would ask whether I saw his brother in the hallway.

"Not yet," I'd answer, "but he's on his way."

Of course, I had no idea what his brother looked like, but I figured I'd see him eventually, unless, as I was beginning to suspect, his name turned out to be Godot.

So I started talking to Mr. U. At first, it was about stupid things like the fact that his name was Irish and whether he thought Ireland was really as green as in the Irish Spring commercials. He laughed at that and said he'd never been there, but that he'd been to the South Pacific during the war. This only served to remind us that there was something else we were both thinking about and yet neither of us was saying.

"I think it's crazy for you to have to make a decision like this," I ventured.

"Yeah," he replied.

"Are they good?" he then asked without warning.

I didn't even blink. I assured him they were the best surgeons I'd ever seen. Of course, they were the only surgeons I'd ever seen. I hoped he wouldn't misinterpret my smile. It's just that my ex-boyfriend had rubbed off on me after all. It was one of his favorite jokes. "Did you like the ballet, sweetie?" "It was the best ballet I've ever seen." Of course, it was the only ballet he'd ever seen. My fingers reached, habitually, for the dangling turtle around my neck and traveled halfway up each side of the chain before realizing that what they were looking for wasn't going to be found anymore.

Mr. U. was still searching for answers.

"What do you think I should do?"

He tossed the grenade into my lap as freely as if it were a red rubber ball and we were playing foursquare. I felt about as qualified to give him advice on this matter as I was to perform the surgery itself. So at first I said what I always say when I'm asked something in the hospital: "I don't know."

Then I smiled at him: "But I'll tell you what I do know. I do know that they're very worried about you. And I also know that when this has happened to other people, they always take them down to the OR. It's not something we think gets better by itself. But you still have a choice, you know."

"I know." He sighed.

Then I asked him what I'd wanted to ask all along: I asked him if he was scared. I'd be scared. He didn't answer. And then he nodded.

"What are you most scared of?"

"Of not being able to breathe."

That surprised me. It wasn't what I was expecting him to say.

"Not getting enough air during the surgery?"

"Yeah."

That's when he became the first patient I made a promise to, just as I was taught not to do. I couldn't have guaranteed anything else about that surgery—not what they'd find when they opened him up, not what they would do to repair the problem, not what the outcome would be—but I swore up and down that I'd make sure the anesthesiologists hooked him up to a machine that would absolutely give him enough air. In fact, the machine would literally push the air right into his lungs, I promised.

He nodded again.

CHAPTER SIX: FORCED AIR

Mr. U. is intubated in the surgical intensive care unit, so he can't talk to me in his raspy whisper, and come to think of it, I've never seen him smile. But there is a certain change that takes place in his eyes when I come to see him. Even after having taken anatomy, I can't tell you what part of the eye changes exactly. It's not a blink. His pupils don't dilate, but it's not more subtle than that. It's as obvious and physical as a change of color or a wink, and yet it's neither of those. But I know it means he's seen me.

Bruce, his nurse, always thanks me for stopping by and assures me it means a lot to Mr. U. Maybe it does, and maybe it does not. I don't go every day, or even every other day—not since I switched teams. Sometimes it's because I'm too busy—for whatever that pathetic, overused excuse is worth. More often it's because I'm scared that I won't know what to say. I've never been good at small talk. I'll take a four-in-the-morning, college-dorm-room, does-God-exist conversation any day, but put me in a room with cocktails and hors d'oeuvres and I'm suddenly quite fascinated by tiles on bathroom floors around the corner, or whatever's up on the walls that I can read.

I once asked Mr. U. if he wanted me to read him something. He shook his head no. Then I felt stupid for asking. I might've wanted someone to read to me the way my mom always did when I was a kid and sick in bed. Who knows how long Mr. U. will be here? It might be like that summer when it took me two months to get through *Uncle Tom's Cabin* in Cyrillic. His chart is getting impressively thick, though not as impressive as his neighbor's. The first time I saw that chart, I thought it was somehow mine. Clearly printed on the front cover were the letters VI with Roman-numeral lines drawn horizontally across the top and bottom, exactly the way I sign my name. I stared at them, feeling like Scrooge, until I realized they weren't my initials at all. It was a volume number—volume six of his chart! Not so long, if you consider that half of what's written in charts is the same information, repeated over and over again. Of course, the other half is completely illegible, so I guess it all cancels out.

Sometimes when I visit Mr. U., we play charades. He motions me over to the bed, and I try to guess what it is he wants me to do. "The thumbs-up sign . . . up . . . you want something up . . . the heat? Are you cold? Do you want a blanket? No, OK. The lights? The volume on the TV? The head of the bed? Yes? OK, good. Now, how the heck do I do that?" I was glad no one else was in the room when I took five minutes to find the correct button.

I'm not the only one who visits Mr. U. He sometimes gets visits from his brothers. I've run into them elsewhere in the hospital, and they have always recognized me as a member of the surgical team taking care of Mr. U. At first, that made me feel good—almost like a real doctor—but then one of them stopped me in the cafeteria a few days ago to ask how his brother was doing. I'd already rotated to another service by then. I had the same question for him. Not knowing what was going on with Mr. U., medically, put me back in my place—as a spectator. I was no longer following that race, and even now, I don't know who'll end up winning. Does the tortoise finish first, or does the air?

My ex-boyfriend has moved five times since I've known him. Each time, some of the items with which he chooses to decorate his walls get put up in the same places, whereas others are retired.

I'm not sure how he makes those decisions. I suppose the retired items are just the stuff he's grown tired of. Why do we choose the things we put up on walls, anyway? My room was always covered. For years it was pictures torn out of *National Geographics*— the kids' version, of course, not the adult ones my parents still have neatly ordered on a shelf. Later on, it was quotations from books—not books by dead white Englishmen or *Bartlett's Familiar Quotations* or anything stuck up like that. I had my favorite ones from Zora Neale Hurston and Barbara Kingsolver and Primo Levi, and some Tolstoy because he's just so familiarly Slavic. I had them up in my room because when I read them, they reminded me of what I've chosen to value most in life, or of a way that I wanted to be, or they just made me feel good about people and the world and how lucky I was to be in it.

This ex-boyfriend I've mentioned never fails to put up his old firefighting helmet, the American flag, and the poster that now makes me think of Mr. U. It is a poster of a long, winding road that goes down a hill and then back up again. The scenery is not particularly beautiful, not like the Irish Spring commercials. But if you look really closely, you can see a little person running up the hill. At the top of the poster it says in plain white print, "The race goes not to the swiftest but to those who keep on running." I don't know why I never thought about what that meant before I met Mr. U., and I don't know if Mr. U. is going to win this race. But last I heard, he's still running.

"Looking at the World from Far Away"

Amy Antman Gelfand

Dear Dr. Vedanthan,

This month I am on my medicine subinternship, and I'm finding the experience intense to the point of being almost overwhelming. Every night on call I have met a patient whose story is completely heartbreaking. Last time it was the gentleman with pancreatic cancer worrying about his dying wife. This time it wasn't even my patient—I was just standing in the ED when one of the interns on my team came up and said, "Amy, you have to see this!"

I knew she'd just been examining a gentleman with hemophilia who'd bled into his shoulder joint. I'd never seen hemarthrosis, so I eagerly went with her to see the patient. Mr. Jamison was sitting on the gurney with his shirt off, his right arm angled awkwardly and draped over a pillow for support. Rising up from the back of his right shoulder was a mound roughly the size of his head. I was stunned that someone could bleed that much into a joint, and when I felt it I wondered where his scapula had disappeared to, because although the mound was firm, there seemed to be no bone in it.

The resident and intern finished examining him and left. They instructed me to stay behind and try to hear his extra heart sound. Once we were alone, Mr. Jamison told me that he'd bled into that shoulder so many times that his right scapula had been entirely eroded away by blood, and the only thing now supporting his shoulder joint was a "pseudotumor," a growth of tissue, which had filled in the space once occupied by bone. It was causing him significant pain, and he was planning to have surgery to remove it. I had no idea what a pseudotumor was, so I decided to just keep listening and let him teach me. "They might have to take the arm," he said, "because the brachial plexus [the nerves to the arm] and the blood supply might get injured during the surgery." His eyes searched right and left as he spoke, so that he only intermittently made eye contact. The way he had phrased it had sounded so calm and collected, but I couldn't help but notice he had said "the arm," not "my arm"—it pained him.

My mind flashed to imagining him with just a stump, or some sort of metallic prosthesis. I felt at a loss for what to say to a person who had just told me he was possibly about to lose one of his arms. I noticed that although I had finished examining his heart, I had not yet stepped back out to the usual interpersonal distance, and I felt as if neither of us wanted me to just yet.

He saved me from my search for words by speaking again. "So it's a lot to think about in the next few weeks," he said. I made some sort of sympathetic gesture with my hands, urging him to go on. He continued, telling me about how he was on a lot of pain medications right now, and he didn't like how they made him feel. I asked him what he meant. Did they make him groggy? Did he feel out of it?

This time his eyes met mine dead on, and he said, without rushing, "It's like looking at the world from far away. Sunsets don't seem quite as nice. And you don't laugh quite as much." It was such a stunning description of a stolen life, medication induced or otherwise. A dulling of sunsets and loss of laughter, medications designed to relieve pain denying and dampening life.

As I was readying to go, I told him I would see him again up on the floor. "Thanks for listening for a minute," he said, which made me feel wonderful and awful at the same time—why was I giving him only a minute?

"No, thank you for sharing," I said, and patted the elbow of his wounded arm before leaving.

They break my heart, these patients; they really do. There's something unbelievably kind about them, even as they are losing something that seems so unbearable to lose—a wife, an arm. I almost wonder if it is the terrible loss that makes them so kind, though the implications of that scare me. Or is their kindness so robust that even their suffering, their pain, does not overshadow it? This is why it bothers me when I hear classmates saying that medicine is "just a job." Because the patients are scared, and often alone, and I can count on less than one hand (mine not cut off) the number of jobs where people will let down their guard and permit you to shield them from that fear and loneliness, if even for just one minute.

With thanks for your support and guidance,

Amy

Early-Morning ED Blues

Kim-Son Nguyen

S HE LOOKED UP, her eyes weary, her mouth sour with acidic vomit. The dangling nose ring again caught my attention.

"How are you feeling now?" I asked, almost whispering, futilely trying to respect her privacy as she lay on a stretcher in the hallway to the trauma area.

"Still in lots of pain," she whispered back, no longer begging. After four hours of writhing with pain and vomiting on the stretcher, she had learned to give up begging to be seen by a real doctor and had resigned herself to accepting a third-year medical student as her only caregiver. Her female companion had fallen asleep on a chair at the foot of the stretcher, oblivious of all vomiting, lacerations, gunshot wounds, and two-story jumps occupying the emergency department at three o'clock in the morning.

I ran out of things to say and patted her pale, IV-pierced arm. She looked even younger than her age. I could imagine myself reporting at morning rounds: "Twenty-year-old female, status post-abortion three months ago, presented with a three-day history of diarrhea and bright red blood per rectum . . ." I wondered if the residents at rounds would ever put a face to my patient. Perhaps they would never place a ring on that young nose.

"I'm thirsty. Could I have something to drink?" she asked again, for the fourth or fifth time.

"We're trying not to give you anything by mouth, in case you need to go to the operating room." I paused. "But I guess you could take some ice cubes." I made a decision that suddenly seemed momentous after weeks of following orders. A strange sense of pride took over, but her pained face brought me back to reality.

"Thank you" she said.

Three o'clock. Then four. Then five. More abdominal-pain cases passed through, with a few lower-back injuries, one intoxication, and the usual few who were verbally abusive. Pains were mixed together; women and men, the young and the old, the psycho and the drunk and the addicts, the poor and the wealthy, the longtime Bostonians and the been-here-three-weeks Haitians, blended together into an amorphous mosaic of human suffering, rage, anger, anxiety. Five o'clock in the morning. Was it really five already? I sat down on a bloodstained green plastic chair next to the triage area and took a break.

Three weeks in the wards and almost three weeks in the ED

have penetrated the core of my soul. I do not know how. I just know that something inside me has been affected, and I am changing invisibly but, paradoxically, so clearly. How am I supposed to feel when seeing an abdomen being cut by a #15 blade, its fascia separated by the Bovie set at forty watts, powerful enough to fill the room with the nauseating smell of burning flesh? How am I supposed to feel when blood and stool from a perforated small bowel overwhelm the suction, flooding the floor of the operating room? How am I supposed to feel when the team stops CPR and pronounces the patient—a husband, a father, perhaps even a grandfather—dead? How am I supposed to feel when my patient cries with pain from broken bones, crushed tissue, and lost hope while I quietly stand by her bedside, equally hopeless?

Reflection seems impossible when the bombardment of diverse emotions never stops. I let everything in, perhaps foolishly, perhaps stubbornly. Everything I have seen remains in me, hiding in my cells, penetrating my heart. I had thought that I would cry, but to my surprise I have not. After twenty-four hours at the ED, I go home and sleep most of the day. Sleep provides the unique luxury of nonexistence and nonfeeling. Then I wake up and return to the hospital, deceiving myself that I am fresh for another day, all the while knowing that I feel the burden of the previous day—no, that is not completely true. I feel the experience of the previous day and the many days preceding it. I love my time in the hospital, but I wonder whether emotions will ever overwhelm intellectual growth, whether tears, when they come, will cloud learning.

I stood up, left that little room. My nose-ring patient had finally fallen asleep, her stretcher still lying in the hallway. I walked down the empty corridor to the radiology department to have her CT images read. Five minutes later, I returned to the triage area. The stretcher was still there, against my faint hope. She was awake again, retching but not throwing anything up. She raised her head as I approached.

"Sorry," she apologized, probably for appearing so sick in front of me. More retching. I waited, savoring this temporary silence. She finally stopped trying to vomit and lay back down on the stretcher.

"Your CT scan shows that it's very unlikely that you have appendicitis."

She let out a loud sigh, even managed to flash a smile of relief. "So I don't have to be operated on?"

"No," I said quietly.

She closed her eyes for a moment. "I'm so happy to hear that."

I stood there, feeling my heels pressing down hard on the Dansko clogs. The CT images were still fresh in my mind. The multiple masses were worrisome to the radiologists and even to my untrained eyes. Of course, I was not going to tell her of anything else. More tests were to be done. No cancer yet, despite the multiple masses throughout her abdomen. No cancer yet.

I walked away from her stretcher. Suddenly I wanted to cry.

Zebras

Hao Zhu

THE SAUDI GOVERNMENT SENT the twelve-year-old boy to Children's Hospital in Boston to get the best medical care in the world. Before I even started my pediatrics rotation, I had heard his story. He was the Toll receptor mutation on the eighth floor, one of the handful of people in the world with this genetic defect. In fly and mouse models, the Toll receptor and the molecular pathway in which it functions was found to be necessary for embryonic development and basic immune function. In other words, animals with this mutation could not defend against simple bacterial infections. I imagined how remarkable it would be to see the manifestations of such a mutation in a living human being. This was one of the major reasons why I had wanted to do a pediatrics rotation at the renowned Children's Hospital: to see *zebras*. Good doctors think of horses when they hear hoofbeats, but they never forget that hoofbeats are occasionally made by zebras. This boy's case was a zebra's zebra. Some in the scientific-medical community think of patients like him as natural experiments, individuals with inborn genetic defects exposed to the light of science. A scientist can spend years studying a mouse that carries a mutation like his. To the medical world, exquisite knowledge and suffering were embodied in that small child.

When I arrived on the eighth floor, I was immediately fascinated by the cases that the team was handling. On my first day, the immunology fellow, who displayed intense scientific leanings, presented the boy's case. The fellow seemed to be completely enthralled, especially when he was discussing how this patient was going to be studied. Apparently there was still a lot of scientific legwork remaining, because the mutation didn't fit neatly into any classic categories. We seemed to be fetishizing a rare bird rather than treating a sick child. To be fair, the intellectual substance was undeniably thrilling. At that moment, I wanted to be in the fellow's shoes.

Several days later, I was on call and had the opportunity to see the boy. One of the female doctors knocked on the door to give the mother time to put on her veil. As we put on our own gowns and masks, the intern thought for a second about what he would say to the mother if she asked what was going to happen. He asked the senior resident, but she had no idea. There was no real therapeutic plan. Without having come up with a good script, we knocked on the door and walked into the room.

It was late at night, and with the blinds drawn, the room took on a ghostly atmosphere. The boy's mother looked at us through the sliver of her veil. There was no telling what her face was expressing, much less what she looked like. I could only guess whether she was hopeful or upset or resigned, given their six-week stay with no clear or optimistic end point. The patient's little brother was also there, smiling and grabbing hold of his mother's leg, conspicuous in his normalcy. The mother approached us like many patients' parents do: as if the arrival of the doctors was really going to help her son somehow. The way she moved toward us and toward her son showed that she had hope left. But looking at the boy, I could tell that there was going to be little time, and that keeping him comfortable was the only medicine left.

He was a tiny thing, barely three feet long, and dark, as if he had been living in a cave for weeks. He was cocooned in a fetal position, with a machine blowing air in and out of his chest. I thought about how cruel the natural world could be. I didn't get the sense that he was in pain, but it did seem that his soul, a full human soul, was suffocating in a congested, ravaged body. He didn't speak, or it may have been that he was too sick to speak, or that he was unable to understand English. But I was glad that we couldn't talk to him; if I were in his place, I wouldn't want to talk to anyone. I would be wondering why the doctors were keeping me alive. What the hell was all this—the doctors, tests, blood draws, genes and receptors and sequencing, what could it all mean? From his perspective, it must have been a sick game. I wondered what was actually going through his mind as his eyes met with each of ours. I hope it was nothing at all, that it was only numbness. It was clear right then that we were dealing with a human being, but I didn't want him to feel like a human must have felt at that moment.

We were no longer in the vacuum of the laboratory, and the intellectual excitement that I had previously felt drained away as we took in the child's misery. It was a stark and uncomfortable realization. He was both a gift and a curse to medicine: A gift because we could learn about his missing gene and its function in immunity. A curse because his suffering was as terrible as his mutation.

The Last Prayer

Joan S. Hu

My FIRST WEEK OF OB-GYN. I am thrown into gyn-oncology right away, and the rotation is fast paced. Our team is always racing somewhere: OR, floor, "the Tower," OR again, then back. Fifteen patients on the floor, and an OR schedule packed from dawn till long past dusk.

The scoop today is that we are planning a total exenteration for tomorrow a.m., *exenteration* being the Greek for "to scoop out the bowels; to eviscerate." Pleasant thought.

Our star patient is Ms. S.—thirty-three years old, married, with a two-year-old baby boy at home, beautiful brunette, young and tan, who looks as if she could be on the cover of a magazine. Except that she has cervical cancer that reappeared only months after total abdominal hysterectomy, chemotherapy, and radiation therapy. She had apparently gone to Bermuda or somewhere for homeopathic treatment in the interim. Her cancer has now invaded the bladder wall and the colon, according to an MRI taken two weeks ago. The total exenteration will remove her bladder, the involved colon, and her vagina, and she will get a new plastic bladder, a reconstructed colon and rectum, and a 50 percent chance of survival. Without the procedure, her survival amounts to a whopping 0 percent. But first we are going to biopsy her nodes and pelvic walls to make sure the cancer has not already metastasized. Because if it has, there will be no exenteration, and there will be no life.

I am thrilled about the prospects of seeing this surgery, so complicated that it is expected to last anywhere from nine to twelve hours. I copy the elaborate chapter on the procedure in a surgical text with the intent of fully memorizing it for the next day. I am going to watch her surgery, since scrubbing in is an impossibility for a medical student on a surgery that is literally done only once a year at this premier tertiary care institution, if that. All the residents want to watch, and both fellows are scrubbing in, along with a general surgeon, a urologist, and our attending. This is going to be the surgery of the year.

I introduce myself to Ms. S. and her family as they wait in pre-op, thinking that it might help her to see a familiar face once she's in OR. In a few minutes, the surgeon and anesthesiologist also show up, and just before we are about to roll her into the OR, the family wishes to gather around her, including us, her caretakers, to say one last prayer. As her husband says the first words, "Our Father, bless us," his voice cracks, falters, breaks. "Give our daughter, our sister, our wife, the strength to survive this ordeal. Guide the hands of her surgeons so that they may rid her of this disease. May God bless her nurses, who are so caring and careful; give them and give us the strength to help her, our daughter, sister, wife, survive. Guide us, bless us, forgive us, and have mercy on us."

And all the while I am thinking, Will this be her last prayer? Are we, feeble as we are, uncertain as we are about whether we can save her at all—are we her last prayer?

I am standing around in the OR, wishing that I might have scrubbed in. Hoping to help in any way. The first thing we will do is send specimens to the frozen lab for surgical pathology. Para-aortic lymph nodes, left pelvic-wall biopsy, superficial left pelvic-wall biopsy, left presacral pelvic wall, third left pelvic-wall biopsy. And I run down to the path lab, hoping for a negative answer. The path resident is rushing around in the small room, freezing, writing, slicing, mounting, washing and rewashing. The wait seems torturously slow, yet I know she is working fast as lightning. And the pathologist, gentle and incisive, says, para-aortic nodes are negative. Hooray! We are one step closer to the fabulous, fantastic exenteration. And I wait a little longer. Left pelvic-sidewall biopsy, positive for metastatic carcinoma. Superficial left pelvic wall, positive for metastatic carcinoma. What do you mean? Metastatic. Aren't we still going to do the exenteration?

I rush back to the OR. Dr. B., our all-knowing, gentle-voiced, all-curing attending, are we going on with the exenteration?

No. The answer is no. It will be impossible to obtain clean

margins, now that she has pelvic-wall involvement, and without that, nothing we do now can save her.

So it goes, I am slowly learning; the worst answer one can ever hear in a hospital is the word "no." No, she has no more chances; no, she is not going to get surgery; no, she is not responding to therapy, treatment, whatever. "No" is the last finality.

They do a little more, they resect a big chunk of the cancer in her colon, but they decide not to touch the main mass fungating on the top of her vagina, because it is firmly entrenched, "frozen," as they say, into the pelvic cavity, clasping in its death's embrace the bladder and surrounding ligaments. So what will she have? A few more months, at the most.

And she wakes up from anesthesia, much too soon. What happened to scrubbing in for a straight ten hours? I had used the restroom, eaten a big meal, prepared for a long watch, everything. We started at 10:00 a.m., and now it is only noon. As she is waking up, she murmurs a prescient, "That was so fast," still drowsy from sleep. And I wonder if she knows. We say nothing. All of us, the nurses, the anesthesiologists—all we can do is look at her, with a silence too unbearable, with a sadness that strangles the depths of my gut. All we can do is look at her and pretend to smile, rub her hands and her legs, and tell her that the surgery is over. I have never heard the OR so silent and so sad, and the air is stifling, rife with disappointment, disbelief, and the excruciating pain of knowing.

The word is that her family took it badly. How else could they have taken it? And the nurses and resident ask whether it might have made a difference that she spent those months in homeopathic heaven in Bermuda. The fellow says sullenly that it doesn't matter now; there's no need to mention that, because it makes no difference now.

Yes, her and many others. The two other patients that I scrubbed in on, Ms. T., a lovely elderly Vietnamese woman so small and frail that you might mistake her for a child except for her wispy gray locks, with a face so beautiful that you think she must have been a gorgeous little thing in her younger days. Ms. T., who has metastatic ovarian cancer, did not get an exenteration per se, but we did scoop out some of her bowels, to put it crudely. But her cancer was so extensive, extending to the diaphragms and deep into the bowels, that our "radical cytoreductive operation," aka "debulking" of tumor, was dismally "suboptimal."

And Ms. H., a sweet elderly lady who presented with pelvic masses and bloating, who also has metastatic carcinoma that is probably ovarian, had four liters of malignant fluid in her abdomen on the afternoon we opened her up. And staring at us were large white masses of cancer perched on top of her bowels, right over the omentum, draped luxuriously like kings. And as soon as we touched the cancer, as soon as we started dissecting and cutting just a little bit, blood began pouring into her abdomen, like a crimson flood. Where was it coming from? And we scrambled to stop up the blood, to find the arteries that were leaking. But alas, it was her cancer. Thirsty for blood, unquenchable and unforgiving. And the surgeon could not help but shake his head time and again, all the while muttering that this was a mess, this was just awful, this was a dirty, nasty business.

And this whole week, I have been wondering: How much can we take out? Can we remove Ms. S.'s pelvis to save her? Can we take Ms. T.'s and Ms. H.'s bowels all out? How much of them must we take away to preserve the meager bit that is left? How much of them has the cancer eaten and devoured, engulfed and swallowed up whole? It seems to me a monster of a demon. The white ghoul that gnaws and devours from the inside out. And we are the exorcists, the demon chasers, the high priests, the wise men. And we cut and cull and slash and sew, scoop and slay, we eviscerate and extirpate, in the hope—vain hope!—that a prayer and a chant, a magical wave or two of the miraculous sterilized wands of our armamentarium, will exterminate the demons forever. But inevitably, they come back. It is so hard to believe, even when the sea of purple cells are staring me straight in the eyes, that this is her fate, as it might be mine. To see ourselves eaten away by such . . . invisible fiends of fate. And what good was the prayer, the last prayer of all? Guiding our hands to extinction.

I heard the Twenty-third Psalm on the radio today, and I wrote it down for safekeeping. I think I might read it to a dying patient one day, if she likes. I think I know now why we say prayers.

> The Lord is my shepherd; I shall not want.
> He makes me to lie down in green pastures,
> He leads me beside the still waters.
> He restores my soul.
> He guides me in straight paths for His Name's sake.

Yea, though I walk through the valley of the shadow
   of death,
I will fear no evil
For Thou art with me.
Thy rod and Thy staff, they comfort me.
Thou preparest a table before me in the presence of mine
   enemies.
Thou anointest my head with oil,
My cup runneth over.
Surely goodness and mercy shall follow me all the days
   of my life,
And I shall dwell in the House of the Lord forever.

It is a psalm of completion, a psalm of fullness and fulfill-
ment. It does what "we" cannot do. This week I have come to
understand that it is a song that replaces what is lost with spiritual substance. Be it true or not, the elegy provides enormous
comfort, for it hints at the eventual restoration of what death
has taken away, and what the demons have robbed from us. It
promises to give back what we could not.

Limitations

Greg Feldman

T HERE IS NO LECTURE during the first year of medical school called "The Patient Whom Medicine Fails." Mr. Colovos did not initially appear to be such a patient. Mr. Colovos had been hit by a car and had incurred extensive abdominal trauma. Removing his shattered spleen and colon saved him, but several rounds of operations and physical therapy left him with lower leg pain so severe that, at the age of fifty-five, he found himself unable to walk or drive a car. Recently he came in with a urinary tract infection and abdominal pain that we could not treat. We puzzled through several differential diagnoses before a computed tomography scan revealed that his colon was now leaking into his bladder from an abnormal connection called a fistula.

Tucked up to his chest in hospital blankets, Mr. Colovos radiated a bitterness that contrasted with his affable manner toward me and the nurses. Since his accident, he had been unable to continue working, and he was tormented by the constraints of his reduced mobility. The accident made socializing difficult, created tension in his marriage, and left him feeling discouraged and, as he put it, "useless." He had been given antidepressants, but they had not made any perceptible difference in his mood. A lucrative settlement related to the accident appeared imminent after years of legal wrangling, but he seemed largely indifferent to it.

"What good would a million dollars do me?" he asked. He viewed the impending operation with indifference, as it would preserve his life but would not restore its meaning. "It would have been better," he said, "if I had died in the accident."

Grimacing with sporadic waves of pain, Mr. Colovos answered my questions kindly and thoroughly. As we discussed his family, health history, and medical frustrations, his gestures grew more animated and he became more talkative. I noticed a disconnect between his increasingly lively affect and the substance of his conversation. Finally I ventured the question that had been troubling me.

"What gives you joy?" His response was immediate, flat, and chilling: "Nothing." Then he paused, and his face softened at the engagingly plump infant in photographs at the foot of his bed. "Except for her—she loves her Papu." We talked about his granddaughter for several minutes before I returned to the question.

"Nothing else?"

"Nothing."

Since meeting Mr. Colovos, I keep thinking how, as important as physical health may be, the work that physicians do often seems almost incidental to the amount of joy that patients derive from experience. A life without pain is obviously preferable to a life with it, but Mr. Colovos reminds me how patients' attitudes toward their conditions may actually be more significant than the conditions themselves for determining what pleasure patients take from existence. I am haunted by words my grandmother once spoke: "People aren't living longer, Greg; they're suffering more."

Surgeons could salvage Mr. Colovos's life, and they may be able to correct his fistula. Unless he becomes acclimated to the restrictions of his situation, however, I am left with the terrible suspicion that, as he stated, it might indeed have been better if he had died in the accident. I have met patients confronting physical challenges as formidable as Mr. Colovos's who nonetheless take vibrant pleasure from life. And this reinforces for me how vital is the work of those who seek to treat patients' attitudes as well as their bodies. I will spend the next few years learning how to make people healthier, and at times this year, I have begun to believe that this really is the calling I am meant to embrace. But patients like Mr. Colovos remind me that seeking to make patients happier may be as important an act of healing as seeking to make them healthier. I hope Mr. Colovos achieves the reconciliation with his condition that he will need to find value in life again.

Autopsy

Christine Hsu Rohde

Motionless, barely warm, almost cold, sheet silhouetting
    post-human form
How many breaths, how many heartbeats ago has it been?
But now, does it matter? Only the answer to *Why* that the
    bunny-suited MDs seek.
ARDS, PE, MI, NHL:
An alphabet soup of responses.
Irony of seeking answers in one incapable of questions
The tired refrain: "Death is part of life."
Wait. Find life in the no longer living.

The details her lungs will reveal, the insight his bowel will
    provide
But without sentimentality: silent affirmation of the
    prosecutor's words.

Radio plays "Stairway to Heaven" as the saw grinds
    at the ribs,
Insides removed en bloc
Maybe the next song will be Jewel's "Pieces of You."

The dissection begins—
Esophagus, stomach, intestines: the stories they would tell,
Not about *H. pylori* gastritis or pseudomembranous colitis
Or other too-many-syllabled tongue twisters,
But of Grandma's famous apple pie, the all-too-spicy
    buffalo wings,
The once-stuck chicken bone and the bystander who knew
    the Heimlich,
The bout with the flu or the night of too many tequila shots,
But they remain silent. No one else can give their history.

So the dissectors move on to the trachea and lungs,
His first words, his last words,
Once-vibrant vocal cords. What songs?
Church choir, opening night at the Met, drunken off-key
    melodies
The laugh: a high-pitched screech, maybe a belly-shaking
    sound
And the cigarettes—black and mottled remnants of pinkness.

Next the heart.
Not just showing signs of too many french fries

But surely pierced by Cupid
And scarred by emotional infarct.
Did it skip a beat the first time she saw her husband
Or heard her newborn child?
How many times did it race with fear or excitement?
Now the ticktock of the internal clock stopped.

On to the skull, through the dura, removal of the brain,
Recall IT, disembodied dictator.
Every thought, every memory, every fantasy
In the palm of a gloved hand.
Gyri once bulging with information, now atrophied with age
Brain into bucket—truly lost his mind.

And so it is with the rest: spleen, liver, pancreas, bladder,
    gonads,
Parts of her, pieces of him, from beginning to end
Full of unspoken history.
The board is cleared
Slices in formalin, slices on the tray, the rest in the circular
    graveyard.
The hope that somewhere the memory survives, a legacy
    remains,
The period a mere beginning to another comma . . .

The Soul—
Where is it?

It Was Sunday

Tracy Balboni

I̲т ᴡᴀѕ Sᴜɴᴅᴀʏ. I entered through the revolving doors of the hospital shortly before eight. The lobby was quiet in contrast to the commotion found there typically during the week. As I approached the main corridor, the quiet gave way to a subdued version of the streaming life of hospital hallways.

A man was lying on a gurney, his mouth wide open and caved in where his dentures should have been. Pushing him was a Haitian man humming a wonderfully sweet tune. Soon after the gurney passed, a doctor strode by looking hurried, annoyed at having to make his way around the gurney, his stethoscope and ID badge thumping against his chest. An old Hispanic woman pushed by with a cart of cleaning materials, seemingly untouched by the busy highway of people moving about the corridor.

I made my way to the elevator, catching the cleaning lady's eyes for a moment as I passed. She smiled deeply, the lines of her face etching a picture of her soul. I caught the elevator as the door was closing, and found four people staring at me blankly. The five of us looked impatiently up at the numbers as we ascended.

Bigelow 7 is the gynecology/oncology floor, and its beds are filled primarily with terminally ill women. The nursing station was quiet that morning. As I waited patiently for my intern to arrive, I noted the number of patients in house, and I was relieved to find that the floor was not full. I took advantage of this quiet moment to pray silently: Oh, dear God, please help me to make it through this day. I am already tired. Please help me to willingly serve you despite my tiredness. Please help me, dear Lord, to give to the patients as you would have me give . . ."

My intern arrived, and I quickly lifted up my head without closing my prayer. And so our day began.

By two the next morning, Bigelow 7 was again very quiet. Most of the fires of the day had been snuffed out, or at least were held at bay for the team arriving at four thirty. What was keeping my intern and I up was a woman whose blood pressure we could not seem to control. All evening we had been continually walking in and out of her room, giving her Labetalol infusions and watching her blood pressure. Despite the infusions, her pressures remained high. It was late, and I was tired. The attentiveness of the early morning had given way to a single-minded approach in extinguishing this resilient fire.

The room contained two patients. The far patient was the elderly woman with ovarian cancer, whose blood pressure was not yielding to our treatments. Then there was the woman closest to the door. She was a sixty-year-old woman who had only in the last week been found to have ovarian cancer. I hardly noticed her upon entering the room the first few times, but later in the night, it became more difficult not to see her. She was clearly in a great deal of pain and discomfort, primarily because of her difficulty breathing. It was evident what was causing her shortness of breath: her abdomen was distended with tumor and ascitic fluid. She was unable to sleep despite considerable medication, and she was continually shifting her position in an attempt to get comfortable. Despite her pain, my intern and I did not attend to her. There was nothing left for us to do for her that night, and so I had accepted her suffering without any sense of responsibility. In fact, I had hardly reacted to it at all. It was not her pain, though, that was so poignant to me upon reflection, although my insensitivity to it is now a burden to my heart; it was instead the beauty of her spirit. Her spirit penetrated the wall of my single-mindedness, which had been erected through the day and solidified by my increasing fatigue that night.

Despite the horror of her condition, this woman's soul was so evidently at peace. She seemed to accept her pain and discomfort willingly and with ineffable grace. This strange peacefulness was what finally gripped me, although I still refused to ponder what had embraced my heart. I was too busy. I was intent on the management of her neighbor's blood pressure.

But at one point late that night, my intern and I could not ignore her any longer. She was now up out of bed, desperately trying to find a position in which she could relieve herself of her plaguing shortness of breath. She became twisted in the many wires and tubes that fed into her, and we went to help untangle her. In untangling her, I managed to get myself tangled up with her and the wires as well. Given the comedy of the situation, we laughed. Between her gasping breaths, she laughed.

The next day came quickly, after a very short hour of sleep. On rounds that morning, I discovered that she had coded and was now in the medical intensive care unit, unarousable. Later that day, the woman passed away.

I immediately thought back on the night. Tears came as I realized that I had spent the last of this woman's conscious hours with her. I had been given this privilege, and I had hardly seen her. I thought about all that I did not do for her that night. I did not acknowledge her pain or comfort her. I thought again and again about our short interaction, when we were both tangled in her intravenous lines. I heard her laugh between labored breaths. I realized that I had probably shared her last moments of laughter. I marveled at the beauty and peacefulness of her soul. I realized that even in her last moments, she had given to those around her simply by her spirit.

I walked through the corridor on my way out of the hospital that evening. I once again saw the mosaic of life in the various souls I passed. I silently prayed. I thanked God for the woman who had died and for the gift of her beautiful spirit. I saw His love in the window of her last moments of life. I knew she was now at peace.

By her spirit, God had taught me how to serve as a physician—not with a heart hardened by the efforts to achieve the task at hand, but with a heart opened to seeing with soulful eyes.

Transitions

Kristin L. Leight

WHEN I FIRST HEARD his name, Mr. R. F. Spratt, mentioned on rounds, I had the very random thought that it sounded like that of a Dickens character. So when he became my patient and I saw him for the first time, I was surprised to see that this name suited his bearing. Most notably, Mr. Spratt had an enormously distended ascitic-fluid-filled abdomen. This, along with his fair complexion, his distinguished nose, and his small stature, made him a perfect Dickensian figure. I could easily imagine him dressed in a waistcoat, twirling a pocket watch, swashbuckling about, while rubbing his protuberant belly. Only Mr. Spratt's oversize abdomen was not the result of gluttony or alcoholic overindulgence, as would have been the case with a Dickens figure; he was the victim of a rare disorder called carcinoid tumor. And poor Mr. Spratt was not swaggering about in a jolly way, as I wished him to be, but confined to his bed in a profoundly sick and stuporous state. He was a prisoner in his distorted body. Every time I saw him, I thought of a turtle on its back; he could barely move, his stomach was so enormous.

Originally Mr. Spratt was not my patient. He had been a "bounce-back" to one of the interns, meaning she had treated him before in the recent past, so he was readmitted to her care. However, when one of my patients was discharged, the resident suggested I start following Mr. Spratt, as he was a "good medical student case." It was so: Mr. Spratt had been found to have carcinoid several years before, when it had metastasized to his liver. He had been treated with chemotherapy, which had been discontinued the previous year because of side effects, and for the past few months, he had suffered from a belly swollen with fluid from tumor invasion of his liver. During the course of his hospital stay, he developed a serious infection of the abdominal fluid and eventually failure of his liver and kidneys. He also had an altered mental state from the liver failure, and a flapping tremor of the hands often seen in patients with severe liver disease. This flapping motion was a favorite physical finding that the residents liked to point out to the students. Poor Mr. Spratt must have started to believe he was a traffic guard, so often was he asked to "stop traffic" in order that we might see his liver flap.

There were only about six days between the time that I started following Mr. Spratt and his death. For each of those mornings, when I would pre-round on him, I would ask his name, and he would say in a ceremonious, albeit barely understandable, way, "R—— F—— Spratt Junior." He never forgot the "Junior," not even on the last day. But he did often forget the year and the place where he was staying. I discovered from his wife that he would study for these sessions, repeatedly asking her the name of the hospital and the date so that he could answer correctly. He was probably accustomed to having given the correct answer most of his life. It was easy to tell that he was an intelligent and dignified man, and it was heartbreaking to see him confined as he was—by diapers, by restraints (he fell several times), and by his own failing body and dulled senses. The last few days, when he could barely answer my questions, I would, after I examined him, stand with my hand resting on his abdomen, watch his laborious breathing, and try to imagine him as he was in his pre-hospital life. I had surprisingly clear, almost movielike images of him: Mr. Spratt playing with grandchildren, presiding over the turkey at Thanksgiving, grilling in the backyard. And this made me feel strangely connected to him, despite his silence and mine. It is said that the comatose are still aware of who and what is around them, and I hoped that Mr. Spratt, in his stuporous, pained, and nearly comatose state, could detect a presence that wished him well.

When I first started following Mr. Spratt, the attending asked me to give a talk on his history and hospital course and to try to explain what was going on with him medically. I had put it off because his case was so complex; it had required hours of poring over his medical records, laboratory tests, and studies, not to mention the literature on his rare condition. When I finally met with the attending one Friday afternoon, I still did not feel as though I had gotten the big picture on Mr. Spratt. I had not, but the attending was able to see things more clearly. He was able to conclude that both Mr. Spratt's liver and kidney function were significantly declining and that his prognosis was poor, much worse than the attending had originally believed.

Strangely and serendipitously, ten minutes after our meeting, Mr. Spratt had an episode of dangerously low blood pressure, and the covering intern, who did not know the patient, called our attending to the floor. I happened to be wandering by when it occurred and was a witness to what followed. After the attending confirmed that Mr. Spratt was stable, he pulled the family aside to talk. The day before this, the intern had broached the subject of end-of-life decisions with the family, who chose to take all measures to keep him alive—"full-code status."

One of the daughters, who tended to be feisty at times, reminded the attending of this sharply. "We already discussed this yesterday. We don't need to go over it again."

"I realize that," the attending said, "and I don't want to cause you any further pain, but I think it is worth discussing again. I just reviewed Mr. Spratt's case extensively, and I have to tell you that I think he is declining quickly. His kidneys and liver are failing, and it is only a matter of time now. If you choose to keep him at full code, he will be resuscitated when he dies. And what you need to realize is that this will not prolong his life significantly."

What ensued was a calm and honest discussion, and the family decided not to resuscitate him but instead asked that he receive comfort measures only. Those ten minutes of discussion radically transformed our treatment plan; the goal was no longer to try to improve his condition, but rather to stabilize him so that he could go home to die. More important, it telescoped the situation for the family. Not only was he going to die, but soon. It seemed to me, although I could not know for sure, that no one had given them this message before or laid it out so clearly.

It is a very strange experience to be present at the most significant moments of others' lives, when you have no prior intimate connection to them. It is equally disconcerting to be in the midst of one of these life-changing points in time and to realize that the world is proceeding as usual around you. There is a wonderful W. H. Auden poem, "Musée des Beaux Arts," that describes the incongruity and loneliness of suffering in isolation while others are engrossed in their everyday activities, as in my favorite line, while "the dogs go on with their doggy life." I was acutely aware of this uneasy coexistence of the profound, the tragedy occurring in their lives, and the mundane, what was going on in the hospital around them, during that conversation, and again, when Mr. Spratt died two days later. It was a Sunday afternoon, and I had been writing a summary of his case, an "off-service note" for Mr. Spratt's intern, who was leaving the following day. She and I had also spent a good deal of time discussing how to present him to the new intern and resident and how to manage his discharge home. Earlier that day, the family had asked her if he could go home that evening. The intern hesitated about it and said she was not sure he was stable enough. I beseeched her, but my motivation was not entirely selfless. I wanted him to go home quickly so he could die surrounded by his family, but to be honest, I was also scared to be the only person left on the team who knew anything about him, especially when he was at death's door. We made some calls to see about getting him the proper hospice care at home that night, but it turned out to be impossible. Frustrated, I went to check on him, only to find that all his family was in the room. Not wanting to intrude, I ducked across the hall to see my new patient. And during that fifteen-minute interval, Mr. Spratt departed this world.

I walked out of my new patient's room to see the intern emerge from Mr. Spratt's room. I asked what was going on, if I could do anything.

"You know he died, don't you?" she said abruptly.

I did not. I grabbed her arm and repeated incredulously, "He died? Oh my God, oh my God."

I do not know why in that moment I had such trouble accepting it as fact. She kept walking toward the end of the hall, where the family was clustered. I followed, but she motioned me to stay back. I felt frustrated, and conflicted. I had a strong urge to go with her, to offer what little consolation I could, although at the same time I was scared to go.

As I waited for her, I thought back to the time when my grandfather died of a hemorrhagic stroke at Duke Hospital. I recalled the nurse who brought us drinks when we were saying good-bye to him; people still get thirsty at a deathbed. I remembered the kind person who gave us her cellular phone—for some reason, we could not use the emergency-room phone to dial long distance—so that my grandfather could say his final words to his son. I recalled the young neurology resident who told us, so kindly and so regretfully, the news that he was going to die imminently. All of these people and these moments mattered. Although these people did not fully share our grief, their acknowledgment of it, their witnessing it, and their concern for us, the survivors, was truly meaningful. I wanted to honor the grief of the Spratt family. I lingered in the hall until his wife and two daughters came out of their talk with the intern, and I stammered that I was sorry for their loss, that I had enjoyed knowing him, and that he was a wonderful man. They nodded tearfully and made their way to his room.

As I rode home that afternoon, the sun was shining brightly, glinting off Jamaica Pond. How precious, brief, and transient is life. My feelings about Mr. Spratt's death were a mixture of sadness and relief. I thought back to that morning when he had a moment of lucidity, roused from his alternate reality long enough to tell the attending that he wanted his restraints removed. "Now, n-o-w, now, doctor, and I mean it. I want to be free." Released from the shackles of his body, he finally was.

Imagine How You'd Feel

Andrea Dalve-Endres

THE EMERGENCY ROOM was overflowing upon our arrival that afternoon, unusually so. Patients were spilling into the hallways, sitting in the halls, filling the waiting room. My student partner and I were sent off regularly to see patients and come back with our evaluation. Upon return to the front desk, we found a distraught nurse who told us to go to the code room; she simply couldn't because she had a six-month-old child herself. It didn't sound good.

In the code room . . . it was coordinated chaos. The attending physician was calling orders, people were running around the room locating supplies, monitors were being gathered, information was being rattled off to the nurse, and in the midst of it all, on the gurney was this precious little baby. As I watched the action from afar, it seemed surreal. The father wailed and flailed his arms, looking very disheveled and smelling of alcohol. The baby's mother arrived and also went into hysterics. Who could blame them?

The medical team continued trying to revive the baby for what seemed to be an incredibly long time—fifteen minutes since we'd arrived in the code room and the heart monitor hadn't bleeped once—until finally the child's death was announced. In fact, the child was likely dead upon arrival at the hospital, but nonetheless, they had to try.

The father became aggressive, punching the emergency-room door, and security was called. Fortunately the situation did not escalate. However, the mother wanted to sit with her child for a while to say good-bye. The attending physician said he would find a nice, quiet room so that she could stay with her child for the time being. Then she asked if it would be possible for her to take a photo with her baby one last time. Hoping that she'd change her mind, he suggested instead that she just spend time with him quietly and said they could talk about the second request a bit later.

How long, I wondered, do you really try to resuscitate, or is there a point when you know it's futile and yet you continue to try? Or maybe you don't want it to appear to the parents that you are giving up? Do you always permit the parents into the room when their child is in a code? And I thought, Sitting with a child who has recently died is one thing, but wanting to take photos together really seemed morbid and probably unhealthy, at least in my mind. But maybe it would offer a sense of closure.

The mother stayed with her child until the evening and was

still there when I left. What would happen if she didn't want to leave? I wondered. And how long was too long? Her child had just died, and I found myself asking, How easy would it be to just walk away?

When the attending had mentioned that the mother wanted a picture with her child, my stomach had turned; something about that didn't sit well. The attending had not yet decided what he would do, and I never actually found out the final outcome of this dilemma. I hoped that the mother would decide it wasn't such a good idea, or that once she calmed down, they could dissuade her, encouraging her instead to remember her child in life and not in death.

Squeeze Hard

Brook Hill

"M<small>R</small>. T<small>REMONT</small>, <small>SQUEEZE</small> my hand," I shouted. And he did.

I live and work in a world of confusion. Although Mr. Tremont's exhausted squeeze surprised both me and the nurse, her discomfort seems to further increase as I continued to hold his hand in silence, dumbfounded and unable to move. Although Mr. Tremont's body was broken beyond the point of repair, his spirit remained.

Aside from him, we all knew what was about to happen. The barbaric trifles of modern medicine had failed, and now we were forced yet again to yield to, although never to face, our own limitations. Now was the time to let Mr. Tremont fly. He would never breathe on his own again. The family had spoken their last words and left. We had done all we could, so we said, and now it was my responsibility to execute the plan.

I can't say that I have ever so uncomfortably written an order or intervened on a patient. Only minutes earlier, I had unintentionally discomfited several residents by calmly yet proudly placing a femoral line in a pulseless patient, a task we all knew they could not achieve. I had done my Harvard teaching-hospital scrubs well. My surgery course director would be proud. Or would he?

I scribbled the orders in apathy, the cool dispassion that reigns daily between the hours of 3:00 and 5:00 a.m., and headed off to sleep. But for some reason, I felt an exhausted urge to revisit his room once more before leaving. Take him back to the light, I thought to myself with eyes closed. Take him by your side, take him in peace. I looked around to make sure no one had been watching, and left. The life within Mr. Tremont was weak, but the life within me was weaker.

It wasn't much later that I was back in the unit, rounding on the patient in the adjacent bay.

"Does anybody want to call the family? He's on his last breath," I heard from next door.

"Someone should at least hold his hand so he doesn't go alone," volunteered one of the nurses with sarcastic unease. "Especially since the family isn't here," added another.

But we didn't. We hadn't the courage. Instead we stood as spectators, separated from the action as if by a thick glass, discussing his junctional rhythm and his loss of blood pressure when the silence grew too long.

"Easy note this morning," I kidded to the pulmonologist.

Now I sit at home in silence, still fatigued, wondering what went wrong this morning. When did society decide to play the coward when confronted by our own image? Why are we all somehow ashamed of what we each know is right? Why can't I hold the hand of a dying patient when it brings not even a flinch to hold his heart?

I am sorry, Mr. Tremont. I have failed you twice. Despite the best efforts of my family, my friends, my teachers, and myself to create a man of virtue, I remain weak. In a hospital founded by people who reached halfway around the world to reassure lepers that they hadn't been forgotten, I failed to reach halfway across the room to do the same for you. I don't know if you still exist, or if I will ever see you again, but if you do, and if we should meet a second time, I will surely beseech you the next time I take your hand, Squeeze hard, my brother. Squeeze hard.

Code

Joan S. Hu

I AM DISCUSSING MY MOST recent admission note with our senior attending physician in his office late on a Friday afternoon when he receives a page. He squints at his pager, then turns to look at me: "Guess what, your patient is coding—right now."

My patient, my patient whose differential diagnosis we have just been discussing. My patient whose family had expressly stated to our team that he was to be "do not intubate/do not resuscitate" in the case of cardiopulmonary arrest. My patient, whose family has suddenly changed their minds.

My mysterious seventy-three-year-old gaunt and frail Jordanian man who says, "Hello, Doctor, How are you?" and "Thank you so much, Doctor," every time I arrive and leave his hospital room, though I am so much less than a doctor (and I think he knows that). Mysterious because he came into the hospital with pneumonia-like symptoms, weight loss, and difficulty breathing from emphysema. Mysterious because his left lung has a huge collection of loculated fluid, and the radiologist and our attending have gone back and forth about whether the fluid is infected or malignant. Does he have pneumonia, or does he have cancer? Drainage of the fluid yielded indefinite results. We had considered obtaining biopsies of the lung itself.

Except that this morning, during rounds, we found that his oxygen saturation had dipped into the low eighties overnight. And his dark skin, draped over his tendons and bones, looked a poor trap for the meager life within. I was so surprised, indeed very surprised, when our attending said privately to our junior resident and me, "You know, it is very likely cancer. I would not be surprised if he doesn't last through the night." And the look in his eyes was knowing, mingled with pain and pity.

How did he know? How was he so right? And how was I to know, here nearing the end of the first month of my medicine rotation? I had no inkling of how prescient those words were until I walk into his hospital room, my patient's hospital room at the very end of a long corridor, in which are packed some twenty people, the code team, my junior resident, other residents and the senior medicine resident, our attending, and what seems to be every nurse on the floor.

It turns out that my patient became breathless and pulseless moments before, and his family in their understandable frenzy and disbelief reversed his code status and changed him to full code—use all necessary measures to regain life. His body now lies on the bed lifeless, and around him lanterns of IV fluids, monitors, and pressor bags are being raised. At least four people stand on each side of him, with one at the head, and the senior resident, running the code, at the foot of the bed. He yells, "Will someone confirm femoral and carotid pulses!" "How much epi has gone in so far?" and so on, while my patient's two sons, grown men, stand near the head of his bed, their eyes red with weeping, looking on at the production in utter bewilderment.

My patient's wife, whom I have met only once, is sitting in the corner of the room, her head wrapped in traditional Muslim head scarf; she stares vacantly at her husband's body on the bed, his body intermittently shocked into motion by the electric paddles, and then she looks down, stares at her hands, rubs them down her knees, and weeps inconsolably.

The tiny hospital room has probably never had so many breathing souls in it at one time until now. I find a chair next to my patient's wife, place my hand on hers, and squeeze her hand and tell her that everything is going to be OK. I think that it is permitted, even in the strictest Muslim traditions, for women to touch other women's hands, and I find that this is the least, and the most, that I can do. I ask her if there is anything she needs, and I find her a box of tissues. And besides that, what else? As we witness the pandemonium of resurrecting the dead.

It turns out that they've succeeded. They are able to obtain a weak pulse and a measurable blood pressure after two rounds of cardioversion and intravenous pressor agents. The code team decides that our patient must be taken to the medicine ICU, where he will receive the best in intensive care to maintain the meek pulse and prevent it from sputtering into oblivion.

Our team, the attending, the junior resident, and I, take the family into the waiting area next to the ICU, and behind a closed door, we discuss the issue of the code status. My teachers, with consummate delicacy and rapport, with all the sympathy and understanding they feel and can muster, ask the family, "Why did you want to reverse the code? What changed?"

Their reply is interesting and takes us completely by surprise: "In our religion," says one of the patient's sons, "we believe that every creature has a time to live and a time to die, and every last breath he breathes is given to him by God. And what we believe is that you are God's angels; you do God's work. God has given you the power to bring life back to my father's body; God allowed you to create and invent these modern medical machines so that you can work his miracles! Our Allah is the same as your God, and you must understand that, for us, we cannot give up on our father until every last resource is exhausted, until we know that God means for him to live or to die."

We are dumbfounded. Here we are, confronted with a modern paradox. During this entire discussion, my attending and our junior resident emphasize, very gently, to the family that this is not how most people would want their loved one to die. That their father will die a slow and agonizing death attached to these machines in the ICU, instead of dying a quiet death at home, as the family originally wished. They explain that he has in fact already died and the electrical pads and medicines have literally grasped him back from the jaws of death, but that he will die soon, no matter what we do, and that what course his death takes, what peace and serenity we can give him, away from the whirring and dinging of monitors and the bleakness of the ICU, is up to them.

But they will not change their minds: they are determined to give their father the last chance at life, however brief that may be. They are hoping for a miracle, and they tell us as much. Except that, except that—we are supposed to be the miracle workers. God's angels.

And as our futile disagreement continues, the ICU resident knocks gently on the door and touches the arm of our patient's wife. "I am very sorry, but your husband has just passed away."

And therein the discussion ends, and we are ushered into our patient's ICU room for the family to say their good-byes to him, and for us to say good-bye to him, our mystery patient whose killer we shall never know. The family refuses an autopsy. Apparently 600 cc of pericardial fluid had been extracted from around his heart in the ICU before he finally died and resisted all attempts at resuscitation, but that fluid was discarded in the midst of the chaos—so now we really shall never know.

"Code" will always hold mingled meanings for me—horror and bewilderment, fear and sadness, helplessness and hope. It still amazes me to this day what faith his family had in us that we could accomplish the impossible; and however unfounded those prayers were, or from whatever desperation they sprouted, I nevertheless felt enormously privileged to have been allowed to share in their despair and pain, in their search for truth, for divine guidance, and for God. We were as bewildered as they; our reasons were only ostensibly different. In looking back, every moment of that conversation was a precious glance through a window opened momentarily only to the privileged few. To be allowed to share in another's anguish is to be permitted the opportunity to see and understand, and to soothe and comfort. What my mysterious patient taught me, about life and death, and what his family taught me, about hope and faith, I shall never forget.

The Heart of Medicine

Annemarie Stroustrup Smith

I FIRST MET JAN BROWN on her return trip to the hospital. It was her first admission since her surgery one year ago. At that time, one of the attending surgeons on the colorectal surgery service had attempted to remove the tumor that was blocking her small intestine. Unfortunately, as the operation progressed it became increasingly clear that Jan's tumor was not simply plugging her intestine, but was completely investing it: gluing it down to her spine, plastering one loop of bowel to another, and creating a twisted, complicated mass made up of both tumor and vital organs. So one year ago, Jan woke up from what she hoped would be her last trip to the operating room and was told that although some tumor had been resected, much was left behind. The remaining tumor would inevitably grow back.

When she was told shortly thereafter that she had twelve to twenty-four months to live, she said, "I'll prove you wrong."

Jan is fifty-two years old. She has two teenage sons. The weekend before coming back to the hospital, Jan and her husband had taken their older son to college. It was a difficult separation, not least of all because Jan began feeling increasingly bloated and nauseated as the weekend progressed. By Monday night, she had begun to vomit every few hours. Tuesday she stopped eating and drinking as she felt too unwell, but the vomiting continued. On Wednesday, she went to a scheduled office visit with her oncologist. He sent her straight to the hospital. That is how, at approximately six o'clock on a rainy Wednesday night in early September, Jan Brown came into my care.

Of course, she was not ever truly in my care. She was admitted to Dr. Smith's team. I, as the third-year medical student, was the most junior member of that team. My responsibilities were rarely more glamorous than wound checks and paperwork, but on that night I was asked to do the admitting history and physical, as Jan had bypassed these steps by entering the hospital without stopping in the emergency room.

I spent much of that night making Jan comfortable. Initially that meant putting a tube up one nostril and down her throat into her stomach to drain the fluid she would otherwise vomit. As the night went on, though, I realized that what Jan needed most was emotional support. She had fought her illness since her initial diagnosis more than a year before and still hadn't accepted that she was a very, very ill woman. We talked about how she was too young to have an unresectable tumor (she wasn't ready to say out loud that she was dying, although she clearly knew she was) and how she was scared for herself and even more so for her family. We talked about how she desperately wanted more chemotherapy, but how that might not be the best choice, as she'd already failed the two most promising regimens for her cancer. We talked about how she needed to talk to her husband, her high school sweetheart, and how he would be strong enough to take it. And we talked about her younger son, who was struggling too much as a teenager to be left without a mother.

The next morning, I called the palliative care psychiatrist at the Dana-Farber for a consult, as Jan certainly needed someone to talk things through with on a long-term basis. I spent much of the next week following Jan to and from the operating room. I had the terrible task of telling her that our last surgical attempt had been unsuccessful. I sat with her husband as the attending surgeon told him that his wife had, at most, only a few more months to live.

The day Jan left the hospital, she was more comfortable physically but in significantly more psychological pain. Despite having lived with her cancer and dismal prognosis for more than a year, this week had been the turning point in which she realized that her death was truly coming.

Amazingly, instead of hating those of us who brought her to this realization, she left me with a big hug and a bouquet of flowers as she was discharged. I like to think that this ability to heal the soul, even when nothing can be done to heal the body, is the heart of medicine.

IV.

Finding a Better Way

Education must not simply teach work — it must teach Life.

W. E. B. DuBois

Black Bags

Kurt Smith

I REMEMBER A STUDENT asking a medical-instruments sales representative about purchasing a black bag.

"Oh, nobody buys those anymore," she responded offhandedly. "Carrying one of those these days sort of makes you a marked man, you know what I mean?"

I'm not sure I know what she meant: either old fashioned or presumptuous, but certainly not dignified or genuine. Nobody advertises house calls anymore either, unless they're some concierge care group that charges an additional two thousand dollars a year for their congeniality. I'm sure that good docs still do make house calls, but nobody's going to go around advertising it. Is it because we really are too busy, or is it because we fear litigation, since you can't take a chest X-ray or an abdominal CT when the patient is still at home? Or is it because everybody's so damned specialized: Can you imagine an interventional radiologist making a house call? Or what about a nephrologist? What's he going to do, taste the urine?

Primary care docs could make house calls. But they're too busy. There simply aren't enough people in primary care to handle the patient load, given that everybody and his dog has to see the primary care doc in order to get a referral to the specialist. And primary care docs have to fill out mounds of paperwork to get paid by the insurance/management industry so they can see even more people on their way to the specialist. Besides that, no insurance company would ever pay for a house call: How could they be sure that the doc is accurately billing his time? Who pays for the time and expense of travel to and from the house? Is there any validated data that show that house calls impart any actual benefit? If so, has this been modeled and tested to show cost-effectiveness? These are the "important" questions that would need to be answered for the powers that be to allow doctors to bill for house calls. And if you can't bill for a house call, why the heck would you make one? And if the rest of your patients found out that you were making free house calls, wouldn't we all be demanding house calls?

I'm not even sure people would want house calls. I can guarantee you that people aren't going to accept that they have an upper respiratory infection without an X-ray, and certainly not without being given a script for antibiotics. Who's going to believe they have a lobar pneumonia without an upright and PA radiographs? Honestly, if you visit people at their house these days, all they want to know is whether your four-year, $150,000 education thinks they should go to the hospital to see a "real" doctor or whether they should just wait it out. And chances are, if you don't tell them to go to the hospital, they're going to go anyway.

At some point, and probably rightfully so, somebody decided that we just know a little too much about medicine these days for any individual to know it all. Ask hospital specialists if they feel that primary care docs know anything about the fundamentals of their specialty, and they'll give you a five-minute sermon on the ineptitude of the primary care practitioner. So we all go into specialties so that we can know it all in our particular field, because that's important. We should know all the details that man has accrued over the past thousand years in order to provide the best diagnosis and treatment. But I wonder how much more we cure people with our specialized medicine. It seems to me that the twentieth century, aside from the development of antibiotics and vaccines, was the century of diagnosis, not real curing. And whether you see a patient in his home with left-sided weakness and dementia and call it apoplexy, or see the MRI and perfusion study at the general and call it a right middle cerebral artery infarct and subsequent stroke, the guy in the bed stays the same, every time. Just because you can call it autosomal dominant polycystic kidney disease doesn't improve that patient's life—it just alters the element of intangible fear.

But we're so confident of our ability to pin the tail on the donkey, we don't even bother to do autopsies anymore. The autopsy rate is down to about 10 percent at most teaching institutions, and most autopsies done nowadays are mandated by the medical examiner. The major reason for this is that physicians don't ask the families of the deceased for permission to perform a post-mortem. When physicians are asked why, they usually feel that the diagnosis was certain from radiological and laboratory tests, and the gruesome process of dismembering the loved one won't add to medical knowledge, won't add insight into the cause of death, and will only add to the trauma for those still living. Yet over the past fifty years, the rate of misdiagnosis at autopsy has remained the same (about 20 to 30 percent for major mistakes) despite the advent of the CT, MRI, ELISA, and every other financial treasure chest of a test that modern medicine has cooked up since the dark ages. Granted, we're getting better with our diagnostics, but we're also realizing that the human body is more complex at every level. I'm not convinced that understanding and diagnosis have been translated into care just yet.

Sir William Henry Osler, that renowned physician of Johns Hopkins fame and literary celebration, died in England at the hands of his family physician. Osler, in addition to writing, teaching, and being a physician to thousands, had always taken meticulous notes on symptoms for each patient, in addition to noting his diagnosis and treatment. At the end of each case, whether the patient was healed or deceased, Osler then sorted his cards based on correct or incorrect diagnosis in order to learn from his personal mistakes. No one would dream of doing that now—what if your "incorrect" pile were found by a less-than-moral lawyer?

Few physicians would be able to make those piles, take a long, hard look at the size of that for the incorrectly diagnosed (more succinctly called the "misdiagnosed," or even the "missed-diagnosis"), and not feel an enormous wave of guilt and responsibility. My guess is that Osler probably felt that same guilt, but somewhere in between his time and ours, mankind bought into the fantasy that physicians always cure and only miss the cure when they fall short of their potential. In the face of striking evidence to the contrary, we still believe (and worse yet, our patients still hold on to) the fallacy that we can cheat death, avert disease, and prevent grief, suffering, and tragedy.

Osler, as he lay on his deathbed, had already informed his family physician that upon his demise, he wanted an autopsy to be performed not only to confirm the cause of death, but to serve as a final lesson in diagnosis to pass on to those who followed his teachings. Furthermore, in the tradition of the time, he demanded that his autopsy be performed by the physician who had cared for him. His family physician later recalled his apprehension at performing the autopsy on such a famous personage, lest he discover something amiss in his treatment or diagnosis. To his credit, his diagnosis was borne out by the duly performed autopsy: Osler died of bronchopneumonia. Today most of us would cringe under some legal "conflict of interest" defense to avoid the harsh possibility of misdiagnosis. When did we stop learning from our mistakes and instead relegate that learning to the pathologists in the basement?

Confidence seems to be a big deal in medicine. I once had a

man tell me, "If you can't be good, you can at least look good!" I used to think that my pediatrician and family doctors saw something when they used the ophthalmoscope to look in my eyes. After a few months of emergency medicine and general surgery, I am fully confident that any doctor who looks into your eyes for less than ten seconds hasn't seen squat, and that when my pediatrician looks into my two-year-old's pupils—while my son shakes his head, squints his eyes, and thrashes his arms—and then determines after a half-second gaze that my son is "fine," my pediatrician is, if nothing else, confident. Nobody wants a doc who doesn't seem to be sure about the diagnosis. I bet Osler pronounced his diagnoses to his ward patients with a grandeur and eloquence that let them know that this, *this*, was a doctor who had weighed the scales of his intellect with their afflictions and come to a conclusion that would dictate their course, treatment, and prognosis. But he was wrong sometimes too! So how do we trade off confidence with an admission of our fallibility? Granted, I don't think too much of my pediatrician's pronouncement regarding my progeny's pupils, but I'd be downright distraught if she simply admitted that she usually doesn't see much in the eyes. There's safety and comfort in ritual and confidence, regardless of how useful that ritualistic confidence is.

So I've tried that suit on, with fantastic results. A confident medical student is infinitely more trusted than one who admits he knows only slightly more about disease than the patients themselves. It's troublesome when I don't have answers—feigning confidence when I'm not sure that confidence is warranted. But boldly I go on, in the tradition of those before me, attempting a stoic, knowledgeable demeanor while I try to learn everything as fast as I can, attempting to merge the mask with the flesh, until at some point I become my own Oslerian oracle, oozing enough confidence to fill a full-length white coat.

But how is anyone supposed to be that confident when we daily reaffirm that there's far too much out there for any one man to know—while family practitioners are ridiculed for trying to treat all disease, and the rest of us hide behind the finite wall of knowledge that can be mastered in a lifetime, choosing to treat specific diseases rather than patients? I wonder who's going to hold *my* hand when I die. I don't trust my family practitioner enough to see him for more than five minutes, the endocrinologist doesn't do hands, the orthopedist doesn't work with soft tissue, and the dermatologist doesn't hold hours convenient for dying. Ultimately, maybe the only one who will hold that hand is the pathologist, long after I care whether it is held or not.

Meanwhile I'm checking the antique stores for black bags.

A Murmur in the ICU

Joe Wright

THE FIRST TIME I visited an ICU was as part of a physiology course. Learning how mechanical ventilation works helps medical students understand the physiology of breathing. So we went over to a nearby hospital, and a doctor took us to the unit. In the rooms of the ICU, there were patients lying unconscious or nearly so, each with tubes in their mouths and noses, the whole unit quiet except for the whooshes and beeps of machines and alarms.

We went into one of the rooms, and the doctor leaned down to the patient and said hello to her, using her name, and then said, "I'm here with a group of students, and we're going to talk a little bit while we're here." He laid his hand on her shoulder as he explained to us that although the patient was sedated, sometimes patients could hear or understand some or all of what was going on around them, and so a small introduction was in order.

And then he talked about respiration, about the physiology of the ventilators, and about the monitors on and inside of her. He pointed to the monitor screen, which clearly showed what he was telling us. I could barely register it. A friend of mine, standing next to me, was in even worse shape. She felt faint and had to walk out of the room to get some air for a couple of minutes. Pulmonary capillary wedge pressure? We weren't thinking about that; we were looking at the family pictures around the room and wondering what it would be like for this woman's kids to visit her here, to see her like this.

More than a year later, I was in another ICU. As an optional part of one of my classes, small groups of us traipse around the hospital, following a young resident who takes us to see patients with good findings, meaning things you wouldn't want to miss if you saw them. So we all trundle into a room and say hello to the patient and then feel his swollen liver, or look at his clubbed fingernails, or listen to her heart.

And so we went to an ICU to hear a heart murmur. The heart murmur was inside a man, a man who was deeply unconscious, who was plugged into machines. There were pictures of him and his family in the room. Did the resident say hello to the man when we came in? I hope so, but I'm not sure; I came in a bit after everyone else. I know I didn't say hello as we put our stethoscopes on his chest.

I couldn't hear his heartbeat at first, because of the sound of the air being pushed into his lungs by a machine. Eventually another student told me to look at the monitor. To hear the heartbeat under the noise of the air, we had to see it on the machine. We looked at a little valentine heart that flashed on the monitor with each beat, and then listened for a sound that happened every time the valentine flashed. Then suddenly, because we could see the beat on the screen, we heard the heart murmur in our ears, as clear as anything, whoosh, whoosh, whoosh. I showed another classmate how to hear it, and she put her stethoscope down on his chest and then looked pleased—now she heard it too.

As we were walking out, one of my classmates looked at the man and said, "Thank you, sir." I berated myself for not saying something too, but hearing her, I also realized that the ICU didn't bother me anymore or fill me with grand spiritual and moral questions. It was a place where sick people were hooked up to machines, and that was that. I was ready to plunk my stethoscope down on the chest of an unconscious man with no preamble, no introducing myself, no ritual of human connection, as if it were perfectly normal for him to be there, and for me to be there too. It was a murmur I was seeking; looking away from the man and toward the monitor, it was a murmur that I heard.

Rewiring

Mohummad Minhaj Siddiqui

Iᴇ ᴇᴠᴇʀ ᴛʜᴇʀᴇ's ʙᴇᴇɴ a period where people feel that they are undergoing a major transition in their life, third year of med school must qualify. In the Transition to Third Year course, a chief resident told us that if we were to stop our education right then, at best we would be highly educated individuals, but that at the end of third year, we'd be much more physicians than not. By the end of this year, our views on the world would be changed, the very experience of riding the T would be forever transformed; we'd see people and walk up to them and say, "You don't know me, but you should get that bump on your neck looked at."

Now five weeks into third year, I realize how accurate those statements actually were.

I was walking down the street today and I saw a man who looked to be homeless, sitting with his belongings in plastic bags, staring at the ground, mumbling to himself. He was smoking and looked emaciated, with sunken temples. I saw him and I swear I instantly took the model of a few other patients I have seen and had a picture in my mind of what was going on with him. On the spot I found I was making up a patient history about him: Here is a forty-eight-year-old man with a fifty pack-year (a pack a day for fifty years) history of smoking now presenting with emphysema and multi-infarct dementia secondary to severe vascular disease. Or perhaps he was a fifty-two-year-old man with an eighty-nine pack-year history presenting with weight loss due to primary lung cancer.

Farther down the street I saw an old lady slowly crossing the street with a cane, clearly strained by the effort and breathing heavily. She was a bit overweight. I was instantly drawn to her feet, which were completely swollen and bulging out of her shoes. I thought, eighty-five-year-old female with h/o CHF presents with SOB and 3+ pitting edema bilaterally along with crackles in her lungs. I was wondering if she was volume overloaded and couldn't benefit from a little furosemide.

It's not that I've learned all that much in the past month; rather, I think there has been an intrinsic rewiring of my thought processes. I've started relating everything we've learned in our first two years to the world around me. Truly I've undergone a transition from a highly educated individual to a physician. I could have met the same people just a few months earlier and thought nothing more than, Homeless man, and Elderly woman. Still I look forward to the next year, two years, six years, when I can utilize my knowledge for the good of others rather than just for my own satisfaction.

Taking My Place in Medicine

Antonia Jocelyn Henry

Five weeks in the operating room and not a black surgeon in sight. Walking the windowless corridors among masked faces and bodies shielded in scrubs, one can lose track of time, not just hours, but years. I knew other black surgical hopefuls had gone before me with success, but that reality took on a more nebulous character each day. For five weeks, the only black faces I saw were pushing brooms, stretchers, and cleaning carts. The job segregation is as obvious as the day is long. The blacks and Latinos who work as unskilled labor pass me in the halls without the cursory nod of acknowledgment common among our races. Maybe they expect me to be too arrogant to speak to them. Maybe they know that more than a short white coat separates us. Maybe the fear and disorientation I feel inside translates into a stern and unwelcoming visage. Whatever the reason, the sense of isolation I feel from the only people who share my features does nothing to counter my insecurity in this alien environment.

Down in the OR, eyes are truly the windows to the soul. Crowded around the OR table with the surgeon, residents, and surgical techs, everyone is clothed head-to-toe in sky blue and medicinal green. Hair covers, clear plastic eye shields, masks, gowns, and gloves sheathe bodies and faces. Body language is constricted and difficult to read. The flat, objective, and emotionless voices shield all but the slightest vocal inflection. But the eyes tell all. Rolling eyes and frigid stares convey all that needs to be said. Standing stock-still so as not to get in the way of the surgeons, carefully placing my gloved hands on the sterile drapes, and being excessively cautious to avoid contaminating the sterile field, I feel like the nuisance I surely am, even though I am the only one paying to be there.

Occasionally the eyelids are not enough to hold back emotions. Above me on the totem pole, the OR techs and nurses, most of whom are white females, exercise their seniority over me by putting me in my place with indirect and direct insults. The situation is only amusing when I remember that this is a temporary relationship. In a few short years, I may be the surgeon taking delight in reminding them of their place. The cycle of hazing and hierarchy will continue to perpetuate itself. I can only imagine they see the future and are threatened by the possibility of a black female surgeon berating them for handing her the wrong size clamp. Not planning to be the kind of surgeon who treats others with such disrespect, I stand by mute as they get their jibes in. Responding would only give them cause to make the remainder of my rotation incredibly difficult.

On the rare occasion a surgeon or another attending finds time to "pimp" me, I start out answering the questions correctly. But as the sessions progress, I become confused, and answers evade me. My temperature rises with my anxiety. I jumble my words. When it becomes clear that I no longer follow them and they have exhausted me with their favorite game of "guess what I'm thinking," my confidence seeps away. I feel as if I am the least knowledgeable medical student they have ever encountered and the first two years of medical school have been for naught. I seek refuge behind my face mask.

Sources of support are precious. My family has been an invaluable source of encouragement and love during this time. I crave the understanding of my fellow black medical students, as they are battling some of the same demons. But we are all taxed, attempting to keep one another afloat as we are pulled by the same undertow.

Last week was especially trying. The pimping sessions during my week in anesthesia left me drained of reserve and full of self-doubt. I couldn't intubate or place an IV in the hand to save my life or anyone else's. Two months after taking Step 1 of my licensing exams, I was still waiting for my scores for a test I was sure I had failed. Questioning identity, purpose, and ability, I felt a sinking sensation deep in my gut. Yes, it really was that bad. And then I was saved. Friday morning, a black female orthopedic trauma fellow presided over my first case. She even invited me to spend some time with her in the OR after she found out I'd already rotated through the orthopedic surgery service before her fellowship began. In the afternoon, my second case belonged to a black male vascular surgeon. Although he did not ask me my name (medical students in the OR do not speak unless they are spoken to), he sent me a message later in the case. While the anesthesia attending was mercilessly pimping me about replacing blood products perioperatively, the baritone voice of the vascular surgeon rose over the din of beeping monitors. He said, "What did Charles Drew do?" referring to the black physician who pioneered blood transfusion. Although he did not acknowledge me in any other way, he made it clear that he was listening and looking out for me.

When I got home, I found out that I'd passed my boards.

God works in mysterious ways. I needed that day as much as I need oxygen to breathe. I've learned that these next two years will be as much about my enthusiasm for pathophysiology as they will be about my stamina to cope with changing environments, my ability to renew my strength, and my trust in a higher power. That day was the clarity I needed to remain on the journey toward taking my place in medicine.

Identity

Alex Lam

THE RADIOLOGIST WHO SPOKE was an older man, a remnant of the all-powerful, all-knowing physician of the past. He wore a blue suit jacket and a red tie and had an aura of confidence about him that suggested that when he spoke, people listened. He was a seasoned doctor, the epitome of what it was that we were trying to become. I listened to him carefully, trying to discern and understand a small piece of that vast amount of knowledge that only decades of experience can bring.

He sat in a chair at the front of the small conference room, lecturing to the twelve students before him. He slowly rose from his chair, his knees protesting angrily in loud pops as his tall frame stood at the front of the room. His voice was a dry rasp.

"Radiology can be difficult to understand," he said. "You look at something, and it all looks the same. It looks the same the way they say every Chinaman looks the same . . . until you get to know one."

What he said next didn't matter. I didn't hear it. My mind focused only on one word: "Chinaman." Everyone around me laughed uncomfortably. We looked at one another and exchanged puzzled looks. Did anybody say that anymore? It seemed so foreign to us. As part of the most diverse class in Harvard history, we were certainly accustomed to multiculturalism and had even taken it for granted. It was sacrilege to go against that system. He hadn't even noticed or hesitated.

I felt this sick sensation in my stomach. It reminded me of the same one that I had often felt growing up in eastern Washington State, in a small town on the Columbia River. It always followed some derogatory statement and grew more intense when the speaker added, "Yeah, but I mean, you're not *really* Chinese anyways."

I knew this feeling. It was the one that I had the day I stood behind the local grocery store. Cowboys stood on one side of the alley, in Wranglers, with wide-brimmed hats and boots, flannels, farm-grown biceps. A line of trucks with KC HiLites, mud flaps, and empty gun racks, caked in dried desert mud, were parked behind them. On the other side stood two black kids, a couple of Mexicans, a half-black and half-white kid, a couple of Asians, and me, a biracial Asian American who had been mistaken for everything from black to white to Italian to Mediterranean to Puerto Rican to Native American to Hawaiian to Eskimo to anything but Chinese, desperately trying to fit in. In times like this, our color didn't matter; we were all the same in that we were not like them. It had come to this because one of the boys liked a girl who liked a different boy, and so that boy had decided to call the other one a nigger.

It was the feeling I had when I stood on the cruise ship with my new friend, who introduced me to his grandmother, who could only ask, "And what do you do on the ship?" It was the rumble in my stomach that I felt when my Mormon girlfriend's parents didn't seem to like me no matter what I did. It was a battle that I couldn't win.

In those days, I became angry and I would lash out. I would fight. I would scream. I would swing blindly at the invisible injustice that I believed surrounded me. I would let what people said get to me. I believed them. For a while, I wouldn't use chopsticks. "Dad, a fork is just so much easier," I would complain. It broke his heart.

Gradually I went to the opposite extreme, taking offense at anything even remotely unflattering to Asians. I could not be comforted by my white mother's comments. "People are just teasing," she said. "Everyone has something to be teased about. The more you let it get to you, the more people will do it." How could she understand?

However, I was also not comforted by my father's perspective. "You will be discriminated against because you're Chinese," he said. "Some people are going to see your name and immediately not like you, no matter what you do." How could he understand? Neither of them was like me, I told myself.

Somehow, though, I learned to use my identity as a gift that allowed me to function in every group and gain an insight into all groups. People would embrace my mysterious identity and accept me as one of their own, regardless of what that was. I heard things that Caucasians said in confidence, and I heard things that minorities said only in their own company. It taught me to have a wider understanding and compassion for multiple perspectives and to try to understand the things that brought people to those viewpoints. However, it was never easy getting there.

Now I sat in disbelief and thought about the conflict I was feeling inside. Should I say something? As a medical student, what power and what right did I have? What would I give up if I was silent? What would I lose if I said something?

I waited until after class, until the usual stragglers had left, then approached the eminent radiologist humbly. "Sir, can I talk to you?"

"Yes," he said. "What is it?"

"I just wanted to let you know that I think you gave a great lecture. It was funny and interesting . . . ," I began. "But there was one thing, and I'm only saying this because I don't think you even realized you did it, or maybe didn't realize what it would mean."

"Really? What is that?"

"Well, my father is Chinese, and when you said all Chinamen looked the same, I found it pretty offensive. I know you didn't mean it like that, but I just wanted to let you know, it really bothered me."

He hesitated. He leaned over and looked at me closely, my much smaller frame standing before him. Then he put his arm around me. "I'm really sorry. I didn't mean anything by that. I really didn't. I was trying to make a point. It was in poor taste. You're right; I shouldn't have said that."

"Yeah, it's OK," I said. "I just thought you should know."

"And I appreciate the feedback. Say, what year are you?"

"Third."

"What's your name?"

"Alex. Alex Lam."

He looked at me, as if measuring my character with his eyes. He smiled approvingly.

"Alex Lam. Well, good to meet you. I appreciate the feedback. Take care."

He turned and walked out the door. The empty classroom was silent.

I thought of that grocery store parking lot three thousand miles across the country, which lay so many years behind me. I turned to walk out of the room and smiled to myself. In that instant, I realized how far I had come.

The Outsider

Charles Wykoff

"CHARLIE, BE SURE to bring some reading material with you to my clinic."

At the time, I did not understand, but after my first day with my obstetrics and gynecology preceptor (the doctor responsible for medical student supervision and teaching) in her outpatient clinic, it was all too clear. About 50 percent of the patients did not want me in the room. It's not that the patients did not want a medical student; if I were a female, they would have been happy to let me be a part of their checkup. It would have been easier just to post signs up around the office: MALES NOT WANTED, or MALES, GO AWAY!

Of course, I can understand the patients' perspective. In fact, in the past I have told my wife that I prefer she see a female gynecologist. But when it comes to my being the one standing outside the door as my preceptor turns to me and says, "Sorry, I'll meet you in my office," I am frustrated. No, I am more than frustrated; I am almost angry. I am bothered by the way the office assistants phrase their questions regarding medical student participation. I am bothered by the fact that the physician supervising me does not do the asking. I am frustrated with the patients for not allowing me in the room even while the doctor takes the history. I am angry at the husbands and boyfriends in the room who interject to say that *they* are not comfortable with a male medical student's being present for the exam of their wife or girlfriend (this happened to me twice in one day). Finally, I am angry at the situation in general: these patients know their provider works for a Harvard *teaching* hospital (or at least they should). If they want isolated, no-medical-students-involved care, they should go to a private physician. How do these people think the next generation of obstetricians and gynecologists is going to be trained?

By the end of my first day of clinic, I feel apologetic for being a male and find myself profusely thanking the patients who allow me to stand in the examining room when they are interviewed. But it's gone too far. I am here to get a medical education so that I can provide the best care possible to my future patients, and here I am, being deprived of the opportunity to really learn how to do a pelvic exam, not to mention how to take a gynecologic history. By the end of the already limited time in my ob-gyn rotation, I will be lucky to have done four vaginal exams and certainly will not have done any rectovaginal bimanual exams. Hopefully my future patients will never have any gynecologic issues that need to be addressed.

Obstetrics-gynecology appears to be a great field. It allows a combination of medicine, surgery, and long-term patient care that few fields can provide. It demands knowledge of the entire spectrum of life: from prenatal care, through adolescence, into the world of postmenopause. However, it is not an option for me, as a male. Obviously men do go into ob-gyn, and some hospitals are actively recruiting men into their ob-gyn residency programs because of the decreasing number of male ob-gyn doctors. But let's be realistic. While some woman may not have a preference regarding the sex of their obstetrician or gynecologist, most women prefer a female. So I have to ask myself, why should I go into a field where I believe I will constantly feel like an outsider?

Before coming to medical school, I was convinced that I wanted to go into pediatric oncology. My sister died of acute myelogenous leukemia when I was a child. Ironically, growing up in the shadow of her death, I never really thought about going into medicine. Not until I entered college and really began contemplating what I wanted to focus the rest of my life on did my experiences with my sister shine through. My career path was there in front of me; all I had to do was jump on.

Once I arrived at Harvard Medical School and began looking closer at the day-to-day activities of the physicians around me, I realized that a surgical field might be the right direction for me. I have always loved working with my hands and have enjoyed sports that require a lot of hand-eye coordination. I've often thrived on experiences that take a large amount of planning and dedication. Also, most important, I have enjoyed my time in the operating room far more than I anticipated.

I have come to believe that my ideal field will somehow combine children, oncology, surgery, and long-term relationships. Fortunately, it is possible to combine these in a variety of fields. I don't know where this will lead me, but I do know that it won't lead to obstetrics and gynecology.

Raincoat

Anonymous

It's 7:00 A.M. and I'm on my way out the door. Keys, check. Phone, check. Palm, check. As I guzzle down my vitamins, supplements, and an antidepressant with some water, I try to remember something I forgot. Right, the morning pep talk. As I begin my daily migration to the hospital, I also commence the daily ritual of tying down all of my insecurities beneath a thick covering of inspiration and self-motivation. It begins to sound a little like a Stuart Smalley skit from *Saturday Night Live:* "I'm good enough, I'm smart enough, and gosh darn it, people like me." You may laugh, but it helps me to get through morning rounds until the next break in the day, when I will repeat this ritual. Pep talk, five minutes three times a day, as needed for insecurity.

At the beginning of third year, one thoughtful physician told us to bring a raincoat to work to shield ourselves against the regular onslaught of pimping, fair and unfair criticisms, and out-right disrespect that we would be subject to on the wards. I took his advice in stride at first, but I have become acutely aware of its importance in the past five months. I've been yelled at, cursed at, told to stand in a corner, had my input degraded, and had my clinical skills openly criticized for all to see. Interns have played mind games with me. Residents have smiled to my face and given me lukewarm evaluations behind my back. Fellows have belittled me during rounds. Attendings have pimped me to tears. I take an antidepressant and see a therapist every two weeks.

The nice voice that peps me up in the morning tells me that this is the system of medical education at a large academic center and that I had better hold on to that raincoat for dear life be-cause this process will make me a better doctor. Meanwhile the nasty, self-critical voice points out all of my mistakes, errors in judgment, and wrong answers and tells me I'd better quit while I'm ahead because I'm never going to be the surgeon I dream of being in the future. That voice rarely shuts up. It goads me into comparing every aspect of my performance with that of other medical students. Am I carrying as many patients as they are? Are my notes as good as theirs? Am I learning as much as they are? Are they getting better evaluations than I am? The noise of self-doubt, self-criticism, and insecurity can be unbearable at times. But somehow it is quiet when I am with the patient, when I am standing face-to-face with someone whose only concern is whether I can help them.

The same interns who seem to take pleasure in insulting my

intelligence are as meek as lambs in the presence of an attending physician. Sometimes I imagine that I have joined some fraternity, only the hazing never stops; the individual spirit has to be broken in order to forge group identity and rebuild character according to the ideals of the fraternity. In its place is a sadistic, nonproductive cycle of competition between equals and nonequals alike.

Maybe there is a method to the madness: how could I be responsible for a patient's life if I cannot survive and thrive in this stressful environment? In the future I suppose that during an operation, no matter the extent of my experience, the mind games and slights I see now will pale in comparison to the questions I will ask myself with each new movement of the scalpel.

My mother always taught me that what doesn't kill us will make us stronger. I remember running to the bathroom in a fit of crocodile tears when she was teaching me long division and I was having trouble. Giving no mercy, she told me to dry my eyes and get back to the worksheet. And that's the day I learned long division. In many ways, third year is the same. It is difficult. There is a steep learning curve. It must be done. And no one is going to hold your hand while you cry in the locker room. Although I have the support of family and friends, I am on my own during morning rounds. So I will continue to pack my raincoat.

Physicians or Escape Artists?

Sachin H. Jain

Working at a major academic center, I was assigned to the care of Benny, a nineteen-year-old with lupus. He had come to the emergency room after having a seizure outside his grandmother's house. Two weeks before, Benny had stopped taking his medications.

When he arrived on the floor, it was clear to everyone that he had no desire to be there. In the first three days of his hospitalization, Benny had tried to escape so many times that we posted security to keep him in his room. When I asked him if I could do anything for him, he always said the same thing: "Get me out of here. I want to go home. I'm not sick."

The truth, of course, was that Benny was very sick. A lumbar puncture, an MRI, a CT scan, and blood cultures had ruled out the possibility of a bacterial infection; the lupus had started affecting his brain. His short-term memory was shot, and his gait was unsteady. Nearly every joint in his body hurt. Benny's aunt had had lupus too and had died from it when she was twenty-two.

In medicine, we use the term *chief complaint* to describe a patient's primary illness. While Benny's lupus was his major disease process, it wasn't his chief complaint. Denial was far more likely to kill him than the lupus itself. While he was defiant and cold in the daytime, those of us who attended Benny at night learned of a different person: a boy who cried shamelessly, stayed up for fear of dying in his sleep, and spoke of taking his own life. In short bursts, he would tell us that he felt abandoned by his birth father. His dream was to become a fashion designer in New York. "Look at my jeans," he said. "I designed them." Together, as a team, we were beginning to unlock the mystery that was Benny. Maybe we were building the trust that would be necessary to transform his view of himself and his disease.

At our urging, he agreed to meet the hospital's pediatric psychiatrist. The psychiatrist put to rest our fears that he was suicidal. Frustration, they called it, a natural response to his illness. But they also added that he needed mental-health care on a regular basis. "He keeps too much inside," they said. "His mother"—who was at his bedside much of the time—"doesn't know how to deal with him." Benny's rejection of his disease had led to conflict between them. Twice in my presence, they nearly came to blows.

Benny's condition and attitude improved, albeit slowly. By the end of his hospital visit, he was less anxious about being there and far less resistant to receiving care. Our greatest breakthrough came just as we discharged him. Benny had vehemently refused to see a psychiatrist on an outpatient basis, but as he prepared to leave, I asked him one last time whether he would consider seeing a psychiatrist on a more regular basis.

"Make an appointment," he said finally. "I'll see how I like it."

The day after he left the hospital, I started making arrangements for Benny to see a psychiatrist at a health center near his home. I called his mother to see how he was doing.

"He's vomiting, but he's keeping most of what he drinks down. The thing I'm most worried about is his sleep. He's not sleeping. I told him if he doesn't sleep, I'm just going to bring him back to the hospital." What about the sleeping pills (zolpidem) we had prescribed? I asked.

"I couldn't get them because they're not covered by his insurance. They need some kind of waiver form. Can you help us with that?"

Of course I could. I told her I would call her in a short while and let her know when I would fax the form to her pharmacy.

I approached the first-year resident with whom I was working and told him Benny hadn't been sleeping and asked her if we could help Benny's family with the form or, at the very least, prescribe an alternate medicine.

RESIDENT: Why did you call him?

ME: I just wanted to see how he was doing and tell him about what I was doing to set up an appointment with a psychiatrist.

RESIDENT: We're not supposed to do that. Once they leave the hospital, their primary doctors are in charge of their care.

ME: I don't get it.

RESIDENT: I know you want to help them, but if we change the prescription or fax the form, we'll have no record of doing it and won't be able to follow up with him about it. Besides, their primary care doctor should handle all that. That's the difference between hospitalists and primaries. We can't be chasing after every person we discharge.

ME (*increasingly frustrated*): But we prescribed the medication. This is part of *our* plan for him. Besides, he hasn't seen his primary care doctor in the two years since he was diagnosed with lupus. He doesn't know a thing about Benny right now. And I wanted to set up the psych appointment while he is still willing to go.

RESIDENT: This will help him reestablish that relationship. Anyway, he should be seeing his primary care doctor, and the primary can suggest a psychiatrist. I know you want to take good care of him. But you have to learn to let go. He's not our patient anymore. You shouldn't call him anymore.

I felt as if the very values that had drawn me to medicine—the sanctity and transformational power of the relationship between a patient and his caregiver—had been devalued in that single, short conversation. I left the room and asked another member of our team if there were any alternatives.

"Seeing the primary sounds right to me," he said.

I asked the pharmacist that worked with our service.

"Next time, try prescribing the medications a day before they leave and asking the mom to get them filled, and try to find out what is and isn't covered."

But we didn't know that we'd be prescribing the zolpidem until the day he was discharged.

"I know. It's hard. Sorry."

Another doctor told me that the hospital couldn't bill the patient once he is discharged.

Tail between my legs, unable to offer anything useful to her, I called Benny's mom back and told what I had been told, that she should make an appointment with Benny's primary doctor. Like me, she didn't understand. She didn't think Benny's pediatrician knew anything about Benny anymore. Hadn't we just been taking care of Benny in the hospital? I repeated the same twisted logic the resident had given to me to justify our inertia. She bought it, or more likely, she accepted it. I went home that night knowing the bottom line of all of this: Benny wouldn't be sleeping that night. It became clear to me that in the eyes of our team, Benny had been our patient, but now he'd been tossed to the next player and was no longer our concern. A simple thing like a discharge order form had transformed us from care providers to escape artists.

That night I called my father. He told me what I had seen him tell his students: always be good to the patient. So I remained in contact with Benny and his mother. I called her daily for a while to set up the psychiatry appointment and see how he was doing. But he didn't get to see his primary doctor for two days and didn't get the prescription filled (or sleep) until a week later. Benny's mom remained worried that she'd have to bring him back to the emergency room with a seizure—or worse.

The promise of hospital medicine is that doctors who practice primarily in that setting are more likely to provide "clinically appropriate" care in cases of acute illness. This logic works if our metric for clinical appropriateness is limited to matching diagnoses with treatment. But what about patients like Benny who are suffering from chronic diseases? For these patients, the prognosis depends more on working relationships than on adherence to protocols. To be sure, all hospitals, hospitalists, or care teams might not have reacted to Benny's situation in the way mine did. They might have faxed the form without hesitation. But what would become of the deeper knowledge of Benny that had been unearthed in the course of his eight-day stay? Or the trust that had begun to enable him to accept his disease? Were they merely squandered artifacts of his hospitalization?

The model of hospital medicine that's being advanced by the profession, supported by industry organizations such as the Leapfrog Group, and reinforced by models of insurance compensation works well for most patients, but does not account for people like Benny and his mom. They don't have the same neat understanding of the separation between "inpatient" and "outpatient." They only have the basic human expectation that their doctors will do their best to care for them. The presence of the distinction between hospital medicine and primary care can create an artificial boundary that encourages physicians, in discharging patients, to discharge themselves of their responsibility to their patients.

In 1926, Francis Weld Peabody famously told an assembly of medical students that "the secret of the care of the patient is in caring for the patient." I wonder what Dr. Peabody would have thought of the increasingly commonplace notion that "caring" is a neatly divisible property of the physician-patient relationship.

The Healing Circle

Chelsea Elander Flanagan Bodnar

—

I SOMETIMES TRY TO GO to the church on St. Paul
Street near Coolidge Corner, but more often than not I am an
hour late or early because I can never keep straight whether the
services are at nine and eleven or eight and ten. Whenever they
actually are, more than once I have ended up spiritualizing with
the Sunday *Times* and a double-tall latte at Starbucks rather
than in that stone-on-the-outside, seventies-decor-on-the-inside
Episcopal church. But on the Sunday after my first month of
inpatient medicine, finding time for church seemed more important than ever. Even though I arrived an hour early, I returned
after my latte to a pew in the back.

In addition to the usual readings, Gospel, and sermon, the
members of St. Paul's were also celebrating the thirtieth anni-
versary of the Episcopal Church's decision to allow women to
be clergy. Coffee hour was also going to be especially fancy this
week in celebration of the lesbian minister's recent marriage; the
members of the hospitality committee had really outdone them-

selves on cake, cookies, and the post-service punch. And this Sunday, like most, they were offering individual prayers for healing after communion. I had heard the scheme explained before, usually while I was doodling a note to my family or boyfriend about that day's reading or making a to-do list for myself of that week's tasks. After communion—which these Episcopalians do in a perpetually forming and dissolving circle around the front of the sanctuary—if you stay standing, the special healing-prayer crew will come to you ready to lay on hands and rapidly anoint you with oil. I had never even considered remaining up there for a second longer than I had to. I preferred to be more of an observer and to stay in the back of the church; I didn't even make a practice of staying for coffee hour (no matter how fancy), let alone awaiting the prayer ladies with their hands and oil to spot me in front of everyone.

But today, the thought crossed my mind. For some reason that oh-so-public standing for a little extra healing seemed, for a moment, not such a bad idea. As the front of the room rose to start the winding and unwinding communion circle, I wondered why I heard the offer for healing so differently this week. I wasn't sick. No one around me was sick. I was elated to be starting a much calmer month. I had just read the paper while drinking coffee for the first time in weeks.

Then they came clearly into my mind: Ms. Huntington, Ms. Mission, Roseann, the first people with whom I had sat as each heard terrible news or waited in the terror of not knowing or gasped for final breaths before dying alone in that huge hospital.

As my turn to rise and circle for communion got closer, tears came to my eyes, and I knew that despite all of the latte drinking, I was still in need of help in bringing this month to a peaceful close. Perhaps, I thought, I was suddenly drawn to standing in front of that whole congregation with the prayer-for-healing team now because I knew real patients for whom I could pray for healing. But in as much time as it took for the row in front of my own to rise and begin their ambling journey to communion, I knew the need for healing was also, and most immediately, my own.

So I stood up there with the communion circle dissolving around me. It took only a few moments of my standing there alone for them to see me. Maybe they knew I sat in the back and rarely went to coffee hour, but the two women—one young, with a dyed white streak in her dark hair, and the other older, larger, in an orange scarf—came close. The young one put her hand on my head; the older one came with the oil. They asked for whom the prayer was to be prayed. I smiled as I found myself stumbling to say that it was for me, and for the whole team really—probably meaning everyone from the team that listens to me at night, to the team that really had the responsibility for the patients that I'd seen this month. The healing-prayer crew was thrown only for a second before they proceeded with earnest prayers for me and this mysterious whole team. I returned to my seat in the back pew. I felt silly. I felt better.

Strong Work

Walter Anthony Bethune

I was the last day of my emergency-department rotation. I was physically drained from the grueling schedule, which had had me working twenty-four hours on, twenty-four hours off, for the past three weeks. I was emotionally drained from the constant stream of crises that make up a typical day in the emergency department. I was even mentally drained, from trying—and usually failing—to anticipate my senior resident's next move and what I could do to help him deal with these crises and avoid, as much as possible, "taking the beats," which was what he called it whenever the surgical attendings or chief resident decided to unleash their fury on their underlings because things hadn't been managed just so.

But I had survived and I was ready for my exit interview, where I would get feedback on what I had done well and what I needed to work on. I remember looking forward to some honest assessment of my clinical skills and some suggestions on how to improve. This had been my first clinical rotation and I was eager for feedback, which I knew I would need in order to become the kind of doctor I someday hoped to be.

But the only feedback I got from my senior resident that day consisted of a firm handshake, a stern look in the eyes, and a surgical comment: "Strong work, Dr. Bethune," he said. Then, as his pager went off, he released my hand, turned, and rushed off down the main hall in the busy ED, angrily glaring at his pager and muttering under his breath, "Fuck! Here comes more goddamned beats."

Had I just completed my exit interview? "Strong work"? What the hell did that mean?! What was I supposed to do with that? Was I so absolutely horrible, such a complete and total disaster clinically, that he didn't even know where to begin and was trying to be kind by patting me on the head and patronizing me with this cheesy one-liner instead of the real feedback I needed? Or had I just done everything, *everything,* for the past three weeks so perfectly that he really had no feedback for me? Perhaps he was just too busy, too tired, too overworked, to notice what I had or hadn't done for the past three weeks? Perhaps he just didn't care.

Since that first rotation, I've gotten to work with many more residents, and I've become more proactive in seeking out feedback about my clinical work. Every once in a while, someone is really able to give good critical and constructive comments. But even so, far too often, the only feedback I get is, "You're doing fine," or "Don't worry about it," or, the worst, "Strong work."

In grade school, high school, college, and even the first two years of med school, I knew I was doing well because I got the questions right. I didn't really need feedback. But now, on the wards, although I'm working my butt off, trying to be there for my patients during the day and fighting the constant uphill battle of trying to motivate myself to read medical texts during the evenings, how do I really know how well I'm doing? How do I know if I'm learning the things I need to know in order to be a doctor and practice medicine? How can I know unless someone who knows what they're talking about takes the time to give me feedback?

But then doesn't this raise the question, who really "knows what they're talking about"? The tired, stressed-out, overworked resident who says, "Be a team player: help out with scut, get me lunch from the cafeteria, and otherwise stay the hell out of my way"? The godlike attending, whom I've supposedly been working with for the past month but who in reality has addressed me directly only once and probably doesn't even know my name, much less what I'm able to do clinically? Maybe the fourth-year med student, then? Or the intern—someone who's a year or two more experienced than I am, but who's probably still insecure in that role and concerned that I might make him or her look bad if I'm too strong? I don't know who I can really trust to give me honest feedback about how I'm doing.

So I suppose I've come back to square one, then. If I do my best, work hard, and try to master the things I think will be useful to me in practicing medicine, then—as I did in high school, college, and the first two years of med school—I'll be able to look myself in the mirror and say, sincerely, "Strong work." On some basic level, of course, I'll have to listen to people with more experience and read books in order to figure out what kinds of things will be useful to know in order to practice medicine; but at the end of the day, I have to listen above all else to that internal voice that pushes me to strive to be better—and that sometimes says it's OK to relax. I have to trust my own instincts, learn not to second-guess myself or doubt that I can be good at this whole medicine thing. Getting good feedback from others is important, but I'm realizing that regardless of the feedback I do or don't get, and regardless of who's giving it, I can't afford to sit around waiting for someone else to tell me how I'm doing. I think my education will be a better one—and ultimately my patients will be better served—if I simply remember to do what I've always done.

The other day I got a fortune in a fortune cookie that I keep in my wallet to remind me of what to do when I want feedback: "Rely on your own good judgment to lead you to success." That simple statement will guide me to being able someday to do truly "strong work" for my patients.

I Would Do It All Again

Gloria Chiang

I REMEMBER THE FIRST time I got to do a whole case in the OR on my own—a simple excision of a lipoma. I remember the excitement of feeling my own hand guiding the scalpel blade through the patient's skin, using the Bovie to separate the fascia, and tying off the arteries as I had become accustomed to seeing it done.

I remember being amazed by the first vessel that spouted defiantly at me and boldly colored all of our masks and gowns crimson.

I remember agonizing about a subcuticular stitch I had thrown hours earlier in the OR that just did not look as pretty as I had wanted.

I remember leaving the hospital at ten o'clock on a noncall night, knowing that I had six hours to sleep, eat, shower, and prepare progress notes for the next morning.

I remember spending my birthday on call, coaxing a patient to drink GoLytely in preparation for his surgery, revisiting a little old lady every hour to see if she was urinating enough with each fluid bolus, and checking a computer every five minutes to see if our patient had finally gone down to get his abdominal CT.

I remember the shocking phone call from a friend who had stuck himself with a needle in the ED and had to start on a protease inhibitor.

I remember my favorite emergency-room chief complaint thus far: "My body is hot."

And here is what I've learned: I've learned that I can handle hundred-hour work weeks without caffeine, contrary to what everyone has told me.

I've learned that people in medicine and surgery really do sit on opposite sides of the cafeteria at the nine o'clock meal.

I've learned that how someone perceives you is often directly correlated with his mood rather than your actual performance. I remember hiding in a bathroom for two hours waiting for a particular attending's shift to end after he had verbally chastised me, only to have him smile at me two days later and tell me that I was doing a great job.

I've learned about the hierarchy that is general surgery. On my first day on wards, I unknowingly sat at the large table in the conference room. A shocked PA student whispered to me that students never sit at the table, but I stayed put, in silent rebellion against that hierarchy.

I've learned to never complain. I remember taking care of a

drunk, homeless man who had maggots coming out of his disintegrating rectum, filling the whole ED with the smell of rotting flesh. When I called my brother the next day, he told me that he had spent his call night wading through bowls of diarrhea with a tongue depressor, looking for a tiny packet of heroin that his patient had swallowed.

I've learned to begin trusting my own clinical judgment. I remember the first time I disagreed with my residents' and attending's diagnosis of appendicitis. After the negative appendicitis protocol CT, I felt the seed of confidence growing within me when the trauma senior announced to the reading room, "She's young, but she's smart."

I had thought that I would find relief at having survived to the end of my surgery rotation. Instead I can't believe that it's actually over. And I would do it all again.

Growing Up

Vesna Ivančić

CHAPTER ONE: PARENTS

"Attitude, Veka, is the only thing that's important," he said.

Because they were on the speakerphone again, I could hear my mother emptying the dishwasher in the background. She can never do just one thing at a time. The tinkling sound was the silverware; I mentally opened the second drawer from the window that faces the patio. The clanging was the pots being placed in that drawer under the stove, to the left of the fridge. The wheels on the dish rack rolled lightly, jumping and catching the rails; it must already be empty. I heard her bare feet approaching on the warm wood floor and closed my eyes. I love home in California.

"I know, Daddy. I'm trying to have a good attitude about it," I said, realizing he had pinpointed my problem precisely, as usual.

My relationship with my father is the strongest proof of genetics short of *Drosophila* and Mendel's peas. We are so alike that he is the only foreign antigen unfailingly tolerated by my immune system. Even when we disagree, the elegance of his logic brings into focus a perspective I needed to have "reset," rather than to react defensively toward. After all, my father is a software engineer whose special talent is to find "bugs" in people's thinking and "reboot" programs. In the end, I am always forced to laugh at myself when he succeeds in reminding me that the big picture still exists. I once asked him how he does it—how he knows the inner workings of my brain so well. He smiled mysteriously and said, "*Ti si ja, Vekica*" (You are me). That is the amazing thing about genetics.

But I am my mom too and was relying on that part of me to be in full swing the next morning when I started my pediatrics rotation. I wish I could be more like my mother, but unfortunately the patient, forgiving, supermom half of me is harder to resurrect. Besides, I was still mourning the end of my surgical clerkship. I could not believe the T would rumble past the Charles/Massachusetts General Hospital stop tomorrow, and I would stay seated, crossing the river to Cambridge. It had been a long time since my babysitting days, and the thought of critically ill children being entrusted, begrudgingly, to me, under the unforgiving eyes of their protectors, was terrifying.

"Just go there and do the best you can, *srećica*," Supermom said encouragingly. "We love you no matter what, and we're always with you."

She had begun saying that "we're always with you" line more often lately, since my uncle had died, I think. I hated it because they obviously were not here with me, and the allusion to being with me in spirit made me think of death—their death. I cannot imagine ever living life without my parents, but I guess it becomes possible in the same imperceptible way that things become impossible—things like believing one can grow up to be a fairy princess who flies and reads people's minds. I do not remember when, or why exactly, I stopped believing that. Now it seems like a simple acceptance of the way the world is. So much of growing up happens subtly.

CHAPTER TWO: CHILDREN

I arrived at Cambridge Hospital an hour early, which, if I had still been on a surgical service, would have been an hour late. We were evenly matched on that Monday morning in October: four students and only four full inpatient beds. I have not seen such ratios since. Before beginning our orientation, we rounded on a toddler with pneumonia, another with reactive airways disease, a boy with viral meningitis, and a teenager with cellulitis from a mosquito bite. We washed our hands so many times that it seemed we spent the better part of the hour in line for the sink.

Sometime about midmorning, the attending arrived holding two purple-streaked glass slides and, like the Pied Piper, led the entire troop of residents and students down six floors to the laboratory. The kid with cellulitis was not getting better—even on intravenous antibiotics—and early that morning, he had developed an ominous rash. The slides we whisked downstairs to ogle were samples of his blood, smeared on the glass and stained and fixed, transforming a little red drop of blood into pink and purple swirls of art. The pathologist expertly clicked the slides into place, all the while looking through the eyepiece for just one or two platelets. Finding none, she settled on the immature white blood cells and proclaimed they were arrested in development—unable to grow up properly. "Still, I'd have to see a blast to make a definitive diagnosis," she told our attending. I looked up from the multiheaded microscope and raised my eyebrows at the student sitting across from me. We had only met that morning, but the look we exchanged revealed we were thinking the very same thing—where else had we heard the word "blast"? And yet no one mentioned leukemia all day. How could you say it in the same sentence as "mosquito bite"? I clung to the closest uncertainty—she still hadn't seen a blast, right?

The attending sighed and apologized for interrupting our orientation, promising she would return after she talked to the family and arranged for a bone marrow biopsy at Mass General. "Things like this don't happen around here very often," she assured us as we stood, filling the heavy room with the scraping of chairs and rustling of papers.

One student was quick to retort that he did not mind such an auspicious start; it was "cool." The Pied Piper stopped in her tracks, the rest of us heaping up behind her like dominoes. "It's not cool at all," her icy voice warned us. "I've known this boy since he was two years old, and now he could die."

All heads bowed to the floor as we tried desperately to avoid eye contact with the beet red student whose shame we shared, despite knowing he had not meant it that way. Of course there was no time to explain. It was just like a movie. We plodded back upstairs for the scripted juxtaposition—a bunch of young, healthy people in white coats, sitting around a table discussing patient history write-ups and call schedules as the attending goes to tell a mother that her baby might die.

Chapter Three: Hospitals

The biopsy was scheduled for the very next day. I arrived on Ellison 18, one of the pediatric floors at Mass General. He was waiting in the doorway, leaning on the frame, one hand resting on his intravenous stand. Suddenly I was not at all sure if he was the same kid I had seen yesterday. After all, I had only met him one time, and he had looked much bigger propped up in bed. I introduced myself again and claimed to bring greetings from everyone at Cambridge Hospital. I do not know what on earth made me say that. "I bring greetings from the kingdom across the river." Who says "greetings" these days? I retreated to safer territory and asked him how he was doing. "A'ight," he said, reminding me he was, above all, a cool fourteen-year-old kid. The kind I was nervous talking to even when they were my peers exactly a decade ago.

"Have they done that biopsy thing yet?" I asked, my best attempt at nonchalance.

"Nah, they're late. It was 'posed to be twenny minutes ago."

"All right if I go with you?"

"Uh-huh."

"So how're you doing?" When I heard the words aloud, I knew I had just asked that question. What now? Fortunately he had a different answer this time.

"OK. They said I'll be here for weeks. They think I have leukemia or somethin'."

"That sounds pretty scary."

He looked right at me, shrugged in that "whatever" kind of way, and then excused himself to use the restroom. I figured he had had enough of me and feared making a difficult situation worse by hanging around with my inexperienced, clumsy self. Bringing *greetings*? My God, I could not be trusted. So as he maneuvered the intravenous stand into the bathroom, I whispered good-bye and headed for the elevators.

With my heart hammering its way out of my quivering scrub shirt and into my throbbing fingertips, I felt just as if I were on the Esplanade for an afternoon jog. What surprised me most was the realization that I felt so relieved as I walked away. That realization led immediately to guilt. What was I running from? Being uncomfortable? Facing death? Providing answers? Providing hope? Weren't these the very things I had come to medical school to learn how to do? The window next to the elevators faced the helicopter landing pad, and I remember leaning against it wondering what to do next. What I was doing—running to class—felt wrong. Going back scared me even more. Maybe this was all wrong. Maybe I could still become a pilot or, better yet, an astronaut? One of those minutes that disguises itself as eternity passed, and I watched my sneakers, in post-call slow motion, heading back to Ellison 18, to my patient.

Miraculously he was still in the bathroom. Maybe he would not even realize I had almost fled. I walked in and introduced myself to his parents. They smiled and thanked me for coming, in warm and welcoming Spanglish. Minutes later, the oncologist called and we headed, processionally, down to the pediatric intensive care unit. The nurse went first, wheeling him toward the same elevators I had just rejected. I followed, continually disentangling various cords and lines, and his father led his crying mother behind me. My thoughts flashed back to my cousin's funeral last year, his friends carrying the coffin, followed by my large family, each person carrying a white rose, the parents holding each other and crying, just as this boy's mother was doing right now. Whose horrible idea was it to walk this way? The kid commanded his father not to embarrass him by joining in the crying. I just stood there, smiling at the mom helplessly.

When the procedure was over, I handed the tubes of bone marrow and blood to the oncologist and took the elevator back upstairs to tell his parents it was done. Only his mother was in the room, and she cried as soon as I walked in. I knelt on the floor next to her and held her hand, apologizing for being seduced by French in school instead of learning some essential Spanish.

"French is harder, I think, no?" she said, and smiled at me. What is it about harder that always seemed better to me? Right then, it just seemed useless—beautiful but useless. I felt guilty about everything. "Can I get you anything?" I asked, knowing I did not have what she needed.

She shook her head no. Her husband had just gone down to the cafeteria.

I told her that she needed to sleep, and eat, and ask for help. She nodded. Who was I, trying to be a mom to someone who truly was one?

I looked out at the Charles River and finally understood what people mean when they say something looks a million worlds away. The Charles was a holodeck image projected on the wall. Its grass and trees and waves and ships and bridges and cars were so unreal and so beautifully useless. As I stood up, I noticed my hand had been lying on her soft arm, my thumb moving back and forth across it, smoothing it, the way my mom had soothed me so many times before. Perhaps it was that familiar motion that triggered my memory, or maybe just the silver ring, like my mother's, that I was once again wearing after three months of a jewelry-free surgery rotation. Supermom had passed on something after all: I have my mother's hands. Hers are darker, and the veins stand out a little more than mine, but not much. We have the same big knuckles, the same long fingers.

How would she feel if I were the child with leukemia, with a fifty-fifty chance of failing chemotherapy, with my best bet being a bone marrow transplant from a sibling, which offered only a

65 percent chance of cure? I headed toward the elevators quickly, suddenly conscious that I was late for class. A fellow student stopped me at the nurses' desk to ask what I was doing there.

"Hey, Ves, aren't you rotating at Cambridge Hospital?" he called out. "How do you know the kid with leukemia?"

"He doesn't have it for sure, OK?" I snapped. "That's why they're doing the biopsy today."

"Oh, is that today? Shoot, I was going to go watch that. Did you get to see it?"

I felt as if I was on *ER,* and next Carter would be asking me how many procedures I had done this past month. My stomach twisted as I nodded yes, unwilling to divulge any more. When I found myself waiting, impatiently, for the elevator once again, it was not fear that waited alongside me; it was a battle of emotions I still cannot describe.

Come *on,* Vesna, I heard in my head. His mom is right around the corner. *Nemoj,* Vesna, don't. But my stomach was already pushing into my back. My breath was coming only in gasps. I hit the elevator button again and again, each time pushing it a little harder. My finger ineffective, I resorted to my sneaker. Guiltily I remembered another student proclaiming recently that he did not want to be the kind of person, "like a surgeon," who repeatedly punches the elevator button even when it is already lit. At that moment, a surgeon is exactly what I wanted to be, and I wanted this kid to have the kind of cancer we could cut out.

But I am not a surgeon, not yet anyway. I clamped my hands over my mouth to make sure no one would hear me. Who knows what horrors his parents might conclude if they saw me crying? *Never take hope away from your patients.* Where had I just read that? Had they seen me, I am sure they would have assumed the worst. Screw the elevator, I thought, and I started running down the eighteen flights of stairs to the lobby; twelve steps . . . turn to the left . . . twelve more . . . one landing . . . twelve steps . . . turn to the left . . . twelve more . . . that's two . . .

Chapter Four: Growing Up

My parents called me tonight. Even my sister was home from veterinary school for the weekend because her college friend was in town visiting. She said something about vertebral fossae and all the reading she was assigned in *Miller's Anatomy of the Dog.* My sister's friend shouted out that he loved California—"God, it's so beautiful; I can't believe you guys grew up here." At least I had a chance to grow up somewhere, I thought. Then it was my parents' turn on the phone. My mother picked it up with the familiar, *"Bok, srečice,"* which means something like "Hi, joysparkle."

"Hi, guys," I managed, defeated.

"What's wrong? You don't have vesnabells in your voice," my dad proclaimed, disappointed. It was his litmus test for my mood. If I had "the bells," it meant I was happy, and by the transitive law that always applies to my family, this meant they were happy too.

I told them about my patient, about his mom, and about leukemia. These are the things they did not know about. Then I told them some things they already knew, but I told them because I needed to say it. I could not stop thinking about the fact that he must have expected he would still play cards with his friends, get soaked in a rainstorm, lick melting ice cream off his fingers, look up at squawking birds, pant triumphantly after having caught a train just as it was pulling out of the station, stop to tie his shoelaces in the middle of the sidewalk, or change the bulb in the fridge when it went out, but that even these banal things he might not experience ever again. He might not ever grow up—all because some stupid white blood cells he never knew he had would not grow up themselves.

My parents listened for a long time and then reminded me of what I already knew but needed to hear again: nothing is ever guaranteed; no one is *entitled* to anything in life; today is the only day we ever have; and the only things worth living for, in the end, are love and family. This kid has that, I guess—a family that loves him—and he has today, just as I do, and almost certainly tomorrow and probably the day after that. Beyond that, who knows what any of us have?

After all, mosquitoes are everywhere. According to an old Croatian saying, if they bite you, it is because you have sweet blood. I rarely got bitten as a kid, and wished my blood were not so bitter. Today I would prefer it if my blood stayed exactly as it is. Bitter or not, I need it to keep right on maturing, even when the rest of me is struggling to keep up.

Epilogue

A GROUP OF MEDICAL STUDENTS and I were walking through the recovery room of a children's hospital, where nurses and doctors care for patients waking from anesthesia. Even though I didn't work there, I was proud to be able to show the students this part of medicine, all of which is central to the miracle of modern pediatric surgery: the layout of the unit, the equipment that monitors patients and sometimes breathes for them, and the highly trained nurses. I could even spot an opportunity, as we saw an anesthesiologist suctioning secretions from the airway of a child who moaned, to illustrate with real people what the students were learning in lectures about assisted ventilation and the pharmacology of anesthetic gases.

The students' reactions pulled me back. They knew that secretions had to be suctioned, but they couldn't get over the doctor's calmness as he inserted a catheter and applied suction. How could someone calmly suction secretions from the airway of a crying child? Here was real patient care, so much more immediate than an exercise in physiology, but they couldn't imagine themselves doing what the doctor was doing. The doctors who intubated—even more, those who cut and sutured—had to be different from them. "Do you have to stop being affected by that to be a doctor?" one asked. "How can I do what doctors do and still be the person I am?"

My attention shifted from physiology to what the students were going through. They reminded me that becoming a physician requires you to do things you've never done before—not just suctioning a crying child, but talking to people about private matters, sticking needles into people, or putting your hand into someone's body. Many first-year students, while realizing a long-held ambition in becoming a physician, feel an unexpected rupture in their sense of who they are. Talking to colleagues, I learned that these discontinuities are soon forgotten; by the end of the third year, medical students have to be reminded, and even then are sometimes skeptical, that they ever felt what these students were feeling.

Over the next few years, I listened again and again as students became physicians. From encounters like the one in the recovery room, several lessons emerged. First, there is much in the training of physicians (and of other health care professionals) that is emotionally jarring, even if soon forgotten. Second, acknowledging those reactions is key to understanding how physicians develop, to humanizing medical education, and to graduating physicians who will listen to how their patients are feeling. Third, students' reactions point to challenges for all health care professionals. For instance, as in the recovery room, how do we provide emotional support *while also* doing a procedure that causes distress or pain? How do we maintain that balance?

IN RECENT YEARS, the kinds of physicians our medical students become has engaged an audience far beyond medical educators. As a society, we are examining what we expect of our doctors. Gradually we are getting the message in the Institute of Medicine's report *To Err Is Human* that the care we provide to the sick in America falls far short of what it should be. We can do much more to reduce deaths and injuries and to improve quality. We are ready to do more. But what kinds of physicians will lead in improving medical care? How do physicians acquire the knowledge, skills, and attitudes needed to help an ailing system, not just individual patients?

The essays in this volume provide some answers. They illustrate how students, as they move from lecture halls to hospital wards, become physicians. They describe what it feels like to undergo (and to seek) those changes. They make us think about the conditions that facilitate such growth.

Despite a rich tradition of novels and memoirs about medical training, *medical curricula* have offered little systematic description of what it means to become or to be a physician and have given scant voice to the experience of the students. A gentleman's agreement in American medical education seems to exclude the study of doctors: medical schools teach the development of microbes, embryos, and tumors, but not, with few exceptions, the development of physicians. Study diseases and patients, in effect, but not yourselves. The prejudice against self-examination extends to case studies: business school "cases" always describe the persons in the case, while medical "cases" usually leave out that part of the story.

The antireflective tradition not only *omits* the study of how physicians develop; it can actively *discourage* such observations. For instance, when medical students talk about something troubling, like being yelled at by a resident, or receiving tearful thanks from the family of a patient they couldn't save, or seeing a mistake that contributed to a patient's death, others may disparage such observations as venting. A student who objects when a homeless person, seen repeatedly in the emergency ward, is called a "frequent flyer" may be squelched with words like, "What a typical med student remark."

The stories in this book break with that tradition. They not only give voice to the learners, long silent, but also illustrate what makes the development of physicians both challenging to describe and important to understand.

A first challenge is to recognize a *developmental sequence*. Physicians who can notice, think about, and use what is going on inside and around them do not appear, like Athena of ancient myth, full grown. They emerge gradually, along paths marked by a sequence of stages.

The process begins when students, in their encounters with

disease, illness, and patients, notice things that aren't in the curriculum, like the tension between caring for a patient and doing something that causes that patient pain. At first they may feel that their reactions are merely personal incidents, rather than a part of becoming a physician. But many students begin to take these observations seriously and to see them as worth sharing with peers. They discuss them, as in the course for which these essays were written, in tutorials that a colleague, Daniel Federman, calls "havened reflection."

Students may also recognize that their concerns point to problems that concern all health care providers, such as defects in patient safety or quality of care, or failure to show respect to patients or providers. Some students take this step spontaneously; some with encouragement; some hardly ever. But some are prompted by their observations to do research on what they have seen, making their observations the starting points for investigation. Others see opportunities to do projects to improve care. Such outcomes represent the best in medicine—leading from personal observation to shared reflection, to study, and to efforts to make things better. Student observations, as well as those of other health care providers, can in the best situations feed the mill of continuous quality improvement. And appreciating this sequence helps educators support students at each stage.

A second challenge that emerges as we read these essays is how to understand the puzzling phenomenon of *clinical binocularity,* which is the ability to think about people, and to relate to them, *both* as individuals and in terms of the mechanisms that produce disease. The development of this essential aspect of being a physician is worth appreciating because medical school has often been seen (and experienced) in negative terms—as a desensitizing, dehumanizing process. Our students' essays depict something different.

Medical training throws students into experiences that challenge their sense of who they are, causing them to revise deeply held taboos about other people and their bodies. To hear about people's intimate problems, to have them disrobe so you can see and touch their bodies, to be with someone at the moment of death, or to examine the body of someone you knew during life—these are all extraordinary experiences.

In contrast to the view of medical school as a time when valued capacities, like engaging with people as persons, are *lost*, these essays depict a more complex transformation. Before medical school, future physicians, like other people, tend to take others at face value. To that capacity is *added* in medical training the ability to think of people *both* as they present themselves *and* in biomedical terms. It is at once exciting and disconcerting to walk down the street, to notice a person with a certain kind of swelling in an arm, and automatically to start thinking of the anatomic features and possible causes of lymphedema.

Increasingly able to focus on understanding the clinical problem and on carrying out the clinical task independent of their feelings, students start to feel (and to show) a quality that awes the public and may, for a while, perplex the student (as it perplexed the students in the recovery room). Sir William Osler, a great physician of the nineteenth century, called this quality "equanimity" (from the Latin *aequanimitas*). Our students' stories illustrate how different is equanimity from indifference or insensitivity.

Does it matter whether doctors study their own development? Don't physicians receive enough attention already? As it turns out, it matters greatly. Physicians who will take the lead in patient safety need to be able to think about what they have seen and done in order to learn more. In the recovery room, compassionate and safe care requires nurses and doctors with the requisite knowledge and skills, to be sure, but it also requires professionals who are not exhausted from working too many hours without a break, who can work together as a team, who are able to tell their supervisors when something unexpected or unwanted happens, and who can monitor their own state as well as the patients'.

These qualities are increasingly recognized in studies of medical error. For example, a recent review of an unexpected fetal death in labor in a teaching hospital took an unusual direction. While the doctors mentioned aspects of the mother's condition that contributed to risk, they concluded that the tragedy was due to poor collaboration on the labor floor and to barriers to communication, such as the lack of permission for a resident to take a disagreement beyond his immediate supervisor. This candid—and heartrending—departmental self-examination resulted in major changes in the obstetric service, including new training in teamwork and a revised protocol governing trainees' relationships with supervisors. The message, finally, is that doctors have to study themselves as well as diseases.

We hope that these essays will help people understand the workings of a hospital and the ways in which new doctors learn. We also hope that they will remind medical educators that students' stories about their daily experiences, far from being merely what students say, are the building blocks out of which students forge developing identities as reflective and problem-solving physicians. As the need for reflection on practice does not stop at the end of the third year of medical school, we also hope that providing opportunities for this sort of reflection throughout the years of training and practice will reinforce the reflective skills that emerge during the third year.

Meantime, we have a hope for our own student authors. We hope that tying their current experiences to the high motivations that brought them to medicine and to the talents that they will use throughout their careers will foster their growth as physicians, physicians who can notice as well as perform, who can pay attention to individuals as well as to disease, and who can make the systems to which people turn for help reflect our best values of caring and healing.

Gordon Harper, MD

About the Authors

EDITORS

SUSAN PORIES, MD, is a breast cancer surgeon, surgical educator, and scientific investigator at the Beth Israel Deaconess Medical Center and Mount Auburn Hospital. She is an assistant professor of surgery and a Scholar in the Academy at Harvard Medical School. Her research focuses on biomarkers for the early detection of breast cancer. She dedicates this book to her loving and supportive family.

SACHIN H. JAIN is an MD/MBA candidate and Soros Fellow at Harvard University, where he has served as president of the Harvard Medical School Student Council. In 2002, Sachin received his BA magna cum laude in government from Harvard College. As an undergraduate, Sachin cofounded a health care clinic for the homeless and was named a John Kenneth Galbraith Scholar. He was awarded an Albert Schweitzer Fellowship to support his work with the homeless, as well as a President's Discretionary Fund grant from the Commonwealth Fund to lead the development of a health policy education program for medical students. He presently cochairs the Harvard/Commonwealth Health Policy Education Initiative in the medical school's Department of Health Care Policy. Sachin was born in New York in 1980 to naturalized parents from India, who live in Alpine, New Jersey. Sachin plans to pursue a career as a clinician, scholar, and activist dedicated to improving access to quality health care. He would like to thank Sameer Doshi, Dr. Howard Hiatt, Ankit Patel, and Sarika Patel for their poignant suggestions on the text of the introduction. Sachin would like to dedicate this book to Subhash Jain, MD, the best physician, and Sarla Jain, the best caregiver he knows.

GORDON HARPER, MD, is an associate professor of psychiatry. Dr. Harper, a child and adolescent psychiatrist, is a graduate of Harvard College and Harvard Medical School. He trained in pediatrics and child psychiatry at Children's Hospital in Boston and in psychiatry at Massachusetts General Hospital. Dr. Harper was the director of the Patient-Doctor III course for many years. He also mentors residents in pediatrics and child psychiatry. In 1997, Dr. Harper received the Award for Teaching Excellence from child psychiatry fellows at Children's Hospital.

JEROME E. GROOPMAN, MD, is the Recanati Professor of Medicine at Harvard Medical School and the Beth Israel Deaconess Medical Center. He is a staff writer for the *New Yorker* magazine, and his most recent book is *The Anatomy of Hope*.

ESSAY AUTHORS

Tracy Balboni is currently a resident in the Harvard Radiation Oncology Program. Now entering a year of training dedicated to research, she will be investigating the spiritual needs of cancer patients at the end of life. She is also attending the Harvard School of Public Health to earn an MPH degree with the aim of refining the skills needed for this research.

Walter Anthony Bethune graduated from Harvard Medical School in June of 2005 and is currently doing a preliminary medical internship at Mount Auburn Hospital before pursuing residency training in anesthesiology at Massachusetts General Hospital.

Anh Bui just started residency in internal medicine at the University of California at San Francisco.

Alejandra Casillas graduated from Harvard Medical School and has started her residency in internal medicine at the University of California at San Francisco. She plans to pursue a career in immigrant health and women's health advocacy. She would like to thank her family for always supporting her dreams of becoming a doctor.

Gloria Chiang is currently spending her fourth year at Harvard Medical School doing elective rotations and conducting molecular-imaging research at Massachusetts General Hospital. She is planning on a career in interventional neuroradiology.

Kimberly Layne Collins spent the summer of 2005 abroad in Uganda working at a clinic for orphaned children before returning to Harvard Medical School to begin her second year.

Joseph Corkery graduated from Harvard Medical School on June 9, 2005, and has elected to pursue a nonclinical path for the time being. He has returned to OpenEye Scientific Software (where he worked during his two years off from medical school). He is currently developing software to improve the drug discovery process.

Andrea Dalve-Endres is in her fourth year of medical school. As she had thought entering medical school, she now knows that obstetrics-gynecology is the specialty for her. She will be heading off to Guatemala for a month to refine her Spanish skills and work with women's health projects.

Chelsea Elander Flanagan Bodnar is a fourth-year medical student at Harvard Medical School, applying for residency in pediatrics.

Greg Feldman has crossed the country to begin his residency in general surgery at Stanford.

Amy Antman Gelfand is currently a fourth-year medical student at Harvard Medical School. She is applying for residency in pediatric neurology.

Antonia Jocelyn Henry completed two subinternships in general surgery over the summer of 2005 at Brigham and Women's Hospital and the Naval Medical Center in San Diego. She is currently completing her fourth-year electives and applying for residency in general surgery.

Brook Hill is a diagnostic radiology resident at Jackson Memorial Hospital in Miami, Florida.

Christine Hsu Rohde completed a plastic surgery residency at Montefiore Medical Center after undergoing general surgery training at Brigham and Women's Hospital, and is currently a microsurgery fellow at NYU Medical Center. After this year, she hopes to get a position as an academic plastic surgeon. She wrote this poem during her surgical pathology rotation in medical school.

Joan S. Hu is starting as an intern in categorical general surgery at Massachusetts General Hospital. She graduated from Harvard Medical School in June of 2005. Her future interest will likely be cardiac or thoracic surgery.

Esther Huang is finishing her fourth year at Harvard Medical School and applying for a residency in ophthalmology. She continues to enjoy writing when the inspiration strikes, usually regarding medicine, healing, and faith.

David Y. Hwang is now a senior MD candidate at Harvard Medical School. He will be pursuing a career as a neurologist when he graduates in 2006.

Vesna Ivančić is a surgical resident studying urology in California. It is her understanding that this will soon translate into saving lives left and right by operating on kidneys, prostates, and bladders. Currently, however, she admits life consists mainly of rectal exams and prostate biopsies, and she finds inspiration, as she did in medical school, in the operating room and in the stories of her patients.

Alex Lam finished a preliminary year in internal medicine at Boston Medical Center and has begun training in emergency medicine, also at BMC. In his free time, he enjoys hanging out with friends, working off the endless snacks he finds at the nurses' station, and traveling.

Kristin L. Leight is a second-year resident in psychiatry at Columbia/New York State Psychiatric Institute. Her interests include mood disorders, perinatal and reproductive psychiatry, and psychosocial oncology. She also has an MA in classics and English literature from Oxford University.

Matt Lewis is finishing his core clerkships and will begin a Zuckerman Fellowship in public health at Harvard School of Public Health starting in September 2005. He is interested in pursuing a career in oncology.

Wai-Kit Lo will receive his MD from Harvard Medical School in June 2006. He is considering a number of career options, including gastroenterology, oncology, and general surgery, and hopes to incorporate creative writing into his career. He would like to dedicate the essay contained in this volume to his parents, Chor-Pang and Christine Lo.

Kedar Mate graduated from Harvard Medical School and began his internship at Brigham and Women's Hospital in internal medicine. He was recently in New Delhi working on HIV and tsunami relief operations for the World Health Organization.

Keith Walter Michael was raised on the prairie in Tucson, Arizona, alongside his two sisters. He studied chemical engineering and the history of science in college and is currently a fourth-year student at Harvard Medical School, hoping to train in orthopedic surgery.

Amanda A. Muñoz took a year away from medical school as a Doris Duke Clinical Research Fellow. She is currently back on the wards completing her fourth-year rotations at Harvard Medical School. She will graduate in the spring of 2006 and hopes to do her residency in otolaryngology—head and neck surgery.

Kim-Son Nguyen has taken this academic year off from Harvard Medical School to study for a master's in public policy with a focus on international development at the John F. Kennedy School of Government before returning to HMS in the summer, when he will apply for residency in internal medicine.

Yana Pikman is currently conducting hematology research. She will graduate from medical school in 2007 and hopes to do residency training in pediatrics. The patients she met were the most effective teachers, about both life and medicine.

Alaka Ray has finished her third year at Harvard Medical School and will be spending the coming year on several worthy pursuits, such as completing a project about end-of-life care in cancer patients, getting married in Kolkata, India, and cultivating a sense of humor about the world. She will then return for her final year as a medical student. Her interest currently lies in the field of oncology, but she will never deny that almost all aspects of medicine fascinate her.

Rajesh G. Shah is currently a fourth-year medical student at Harvard Medical School and plans to pursue a residency in anesthesiology with the goal of practicing pain management. He hopes to better the lives of his patients by treating their pain, advocating for increased awareness of pain-related issues in medical practice, and working toward the destigmatization of the use of pain medication. His future professional goals include further writing and the integration of novel computer technologies into medical practice. He is particularly grateful for his loving family, without whose support nothing would be possible.

Mohummad Minhaj Siddiqui is a fourth-year medical student in the Harvard-MIT Division of Health Sciences and Technology. He plans to apply for residency in urology with a concurrent academic interest in kidney tissue engineering research. When not in the hospital, he enjoys sleeping, with the occasional interest in skiing and kayaking.

Kurt Smith, MD, completed his degree with honors in June 2005 and is currently a resident in emergency medicine at University Hospital in Cincinnati, Ohio, where he continues to both learn and reflect on the art and practice of medicine and work as a full-time husband and father.

Annemarie Stroustrup Smith graduated magna cum laude from Harvard Medical School and the Harvard-MIT Division of Health Sciences and Technology in 2005. She is completing her residency in pediatrics at the Kravis Children's Hospital at the Mount Sinai Medical Center in New York City. She lives in Manhattan with her husband and daughter.

Yetsa Kehinde Tuakli-Wosornu is a fourth-year medical student, recently named Stanley J. Sarnoff Fellow. Over the next year, she will be conducting cardiovascular research under the auspices of the fellowship.

Ari Wassner graduated from Harvard Medical School and began his internship in pediatrics at Children's Hospital Boston. He lives in Cambridge.

Mike Westerhaus completed his third year of medical school at Harvard Medical School. He spent two months doing a clinical rotation and anthropological fieldwork at a hospital in northern Uganda. This past academic year, he completed a master's in medical anthropology at Harvard and wrote a thesis on the competing theories of HIV transmission and how ideology plays into the formation of those theories. He drew heavily on his experiences in northern Uganda, which has been at war for eighteen years. He has returned to HMS for his fourth year of medical school and will graduate in June 2006. He then plans to start a residency in internal medicine.

Joe Wright is a fourth-year student who can often be heard as a commentator for National Public Radio's *All Things Considered.* He spent his third year of medical school as one of a group of eight Harvard Medical School students in a pilot program that emphasized longitudinal relationships with patients and teachers. He is currently planning a range of clinical electives, from trauma surgery to psychiatry, and intends to make his fourth year into two years.

Charles Wykoff is an internal medicine resident at the Brigham and Women's Hospital in Boston. He will be moving to Miami, Florida, in June 2006 to begin his ophthalmology residency at the Bascom Palmer Eye Institute. He and his wife are also in the midst of being new parents, raising their daughter, Julia.

Hao Zhu is currently an internal medicine resident at UCSF.

Acknowledgments

THE EDITORS WOULD LIKE TO THANK all the students who were willing to share their very personal and meaningful essays. And we are indebted to Kathy Pories, our wonderful editor at Algonquin, for her wisdom and patience.

Permissions